# MOUNTAIN

### International Distress Signal
*(To be used in emergency only)*
Six blasts on a whistle (and flashes with a torch after dark) spaced evenly for one minute, followed by a minute's pause. Repeat until an answer is received. The response is three signals per minute followed by a minute's pause.

The following signals are used to communicate with a helicopter:

**Help needed:**
raise both arms above head to form a 'V'

**Help not required:**
raise one arm above head, extend other arm downward

**Note:** *mountain rescue can be very expensive – be adequately insured*

# WALKING THE FRENCH ALPS: GR5

*Looking to the Rochers de Fiz and Pointe d'Anterne from the final approaches to Col d'Anterne (Stage 1)*

# WALKING THE
# FRENCH ALPS: GR5

by

**Martin Collins**

CICERONE PRESS
2 POLICE SQUARE, MILNTHORPE,
CUMBRIA LA7 7PY
www.cicerone.co.uk

© Martin Collins
ISBN 1 85284 326 8
First edition 1984
Reprinted 1987
Revised edition 1992
Second edition 2001

## ABOUT THE AUTHOR

Martin Collins is a freelance author, photo-journalist and cartographer, as well as a regular contributor to the UK outdoor media. First walking the GR5 in 1981 kindled a passion for the French Alps that remains as strong as ever. He has since written over twenty books for walkers embracing the coast, mountains and countryside of the UK and parts of Europe. He has three children, and lives in north Wales on the edge of the Snowdonia National Park.

**Other Cicerone guidebooks by Martin Collins**

Chamonix – Mont-Blanc
Alta Via – High Level Walks in the
   Dolomites
The Pennine Way
North Yorks Moors

The Teesdale Way
South West Way
A Walker's Guide to the Isle of
   Wight (with Norman Birch)

### Advice to Readers

Readers are advised that while every effort is taken by the author to ensure the accuracy of this guidebook, changes can occur which may affect the contents. It is advisable to check locally on transport, accommodation, shops, etc, but even rights of way can be altered. The publisher would welcome notes of any such changes.

Front cover: *Approaching the remote Pas de la Cavale, Alpes-de-Haute-Provence*

# CONTENTS

## KEY TO MAPS

|  |  |
|--------|---------|
| ▬ ▬ ▬ ▬ ▬ | GR5 |
| △ | MOUNTAIN FEATURE |
| ∼GIFFRE∼ | RIVER |
| ◆ | WATER |
| ═N5═ | ROAD |
| ┼┼┼┼┼┼┼ | RAILWAY |
| ┬┬┬┬┬┬ | CABLE-CAR |
| ○ SIXT | TOWN OR VILLAGE |
| · · · · · · · · · | FRONTIER |

# INTRODUCTION

## The 'GR' System and National Parks

France is richly endowed with a network of walking paths (*sentiers*), from local footpaths, ancient drove roads and pilgrim routes to full-blown long-distance trails called 'GRs' (short for Sentiers de Grande Randonnée). GR routes and their variants are numbered and waymarked and cross all regions of France, providing walkers with an enormous choice of terrain and length of route.

The official body overseeing development, waymarking and main-tenance of these trails is the Fédération Française de la Randonnée Pédestre – Comité National des Sentiers de Grande Randonnée (CNSGR), who also publish topoguides in French.

Some GR trails form part of longer European routes (prefixed 'E') and GR5 itself falls into this category (being E2). Its northern terminus is not actually Lac Léman (Lake Geneva), where our traverse of the French Alps begins, but Ostend on the Belgian coast, or alternatively Bergen-op-Zoom in Holland. It then passes through the Ardennes in Belgium, across Luxembourg, through the Vosges, Jura and Alps of France to Nice on the Mediterranean coast – a total length of 2083 kilometres (1294 miles)! La Grande Traversée des Alpes, with which this guide is concerned, spans just over 660 kilometres (400 miles) and if walked in one linear journey, ignoring variants, is unlikely to take the fit walker less than four weeks. The potential for shorter expedi-tions, or even circular 'tours' based around GR5, is almost infinite, however. One could walk GR5 in shorter sections of a week or two's duration, or use several centres as a basis for exploring regions by day-walking. The scope of excursions can be varied and extended by taking public transport or cable-car to reach the best scenery quickly or to visit towns, villages and sites of special interest off the main trail. People everywhere are friendly, the scenery magnificent and the flora and fauna rich with variety, from the forests and flower-choked meadows in the north to the dry, rocky ridges and aromatic air of the south.

In 1960, a law was passed in France which initiated the setting up of National Parks, mainly as a conservation measure against the threats posed by commercial interests and general misuse to areas of great natural beauty and scientific value. GR5 passes through two such parks, the Vanoise and the Mercantour, and through the Queyras Regional Park. Whilst walkers in the parks are confronted by numerous restrictions (e.g. no dogs, no camping, in the Vanoise), the overriding advantage for everyone is a protected, pollution-free environment in which alpine flora and creatures like marmots and chamois can exist in their wild state for us to observe and admire.

The GR5 Traverse of the French Alps is one of the classic long-distance walking trails in the whole of Europe, and justly so.

## Travelling to the Alps

Private vehicles can reach any region suitable for walking expeditions by using France's excellent network of autoroutes (A), trunk (N) and minor (D) roads; access points appear in the route guide (main section of the book).

Good public transport links exist between Britain and the start and finish of the GR5 Traverse of the French Alps as well as with several intermediate points. French trains (SNCF – Société National de Chemin de Fer) are fast, efficient and relatively cheap, being heavily subsidised by the state. Booking through from Britain to a French destination using cross-channel ferries or the channel tunnel provides a straightforward journey, with overnight couchette or sleeping-car accommodation available. (Book well in advance for travel during July and August and enquire whether you are eligible for any discounted fare offer). Some long-distance services may be boarded at the French channel port and not left until your main-line station is reached, several hundred miles to the south. Trains are numbered and have destination signs on carriages, thus removing much of the uncertainty from changing.

France's high-speed passenger train, the TGV (Train à Grande Vitesse) whisks you along at 160 mph, taking just over two and a half hours from Paris to Lyon and five and a half hours to Marseilles (for Nice). The Paris to Geneva TGV may be left at Bellegarde to change for Thonon-les-Bains, an alternative start for GR5. Reservations on the TGV are compulsory and there is a fare supplement at peak season, but some might consider the shorter journey time and comfort worth paying extra for.

Other stations reached from Paris and strategic to GR5 include:

- MONTREUX – for Saint-Gingolph or Thonon-les-Bains by lake steamer
- ANNEMASSE – for Samoëns
- SALLANCHES – for les Contamines
- ST. GERVAIS-LE-FAYET – for Les Houches and Chamonix
- MOUTIERS – for Pralognan-le-Vanoise
- BOURG-SAINT-MAURICE – for the Vanoise, Tignes and Val d'Isère
- MODANE for the Arc valley
- BRIANÇON – for the Queyras Regional Park
- NICE – for the Tinée valley and Alpes-Maritimes.

Buses often connect these stations with towns and villages on or near GR5. There are few long-distance coach services in France but local buses are generally good and give access to some quite remote places.

The quickest way to or from Geneva and Nice is, of course, by air. Scheduled services are operated by British Airways and Air France, leaving from Heathrow and Manchester. Enquire at your local travel agent.

## Accommodation

Apart from lightweight camping and bivouacing (not a favourite with the French!), overnight accommodation available to the walker on GR5 consists principally of three kinds – refuges, shelters (*abris*), *gîtes d'étape* and hotels or inns.

Mostly owned by Club Alpin Français or Touring Club de France, refuges are often, though not always, located in high mountain country, offering accommodation to walkers and climbers ranging from the almost hotel-like to the crude, and priced accordingly! They can be noisy and cramped in mid-season (July and August) but put a roof over your head when you most need one and provide what some would call a 'colourful' experience! Early arrival for the individual or couple will usually secure a place for the night on a 'first-come, first-served' basis, but groups should try to make a reservation. Some refuges are un-manned and contain only rudimentary cooking facilities and mattresses. Other have a resident guardian, sometimes with family, who will supply food and drink and cook meals. Even so, it is best to take along your own meat or favourite food as the choice can be fairly basic and even the expected hot meal might not materialise! Some refuges close during winter. There are reductions in overnight fees (where these apply) for members of clubs affiliated to those who own the refuges, roughly equivalent to a third of the cost. The British Mountaineering Council can supply details of this scheme. All refuges on or near GR5, along with their specifications, are noted in this guide. (Details are accurate at the time of going to press, but may change.)

As GR5 wends its way over high meadows and mountainsides en route for valley or col, it passes numerous barns and ancient chalets, some collapsed through neglect, some abandoned but intact, if a little draughty, others still in good repair and used by farmers. If caught out some distance from a refuge or *gîte*, such buildings can provide shelter, but never force an entry and take extra care not to cause damage.

*Gîtes d'étape* (not to be confused with *gîtes* – rented holiday homes) are similar to our Youth Hostels but less formal and do not require membership of an organisation. They range in quality from converted stables to parts of large hotels and are owned variously by farmers or local communes. Sleeping arrangements are usually in dormitories, on bunks or mattresses on the floor (pillows and blankets provided but you will need your own bag) and there will be a common-room, kitchen, lavatories and bathroom, perhaps with shower. Maximum stay is usually three nights and many are self-catering although sometimes the warden will cook meals. Booking ahead is advisable at peak season, or arrive as early as you can, say before 5 pm. For up-to-date prices and availability of *gîtes d'étape* (many are closed out of season), consult the local Syndicat d'Initiative. All *gîtes d'étape* on or near GR5 are noted in this guide. CNSGR are aiming to establish a continuous chain of *gîtes d'étape*, three or four hours' walking distance apart, along all GR trails. There are gaps at present on GR5 but these can usually be filled by using refuges or hotels and inns.

Lists of hotels, *logis* (smaller family hotels) and *auberges* (simpler, cheaper inns) are available for all areas from the French Government Tourist Office, 178 Piccadilly, London W1. It is customary to inspect the offered room first, having checked the displayed price, and you might be expected to eat on the premises too. Establishments are star graded, much as in this country.

A visit to the Syndicat d'Initiative on arrival at a town will yield details of hotels, prices and sometimes vacancies. If there are no hotels or inns, try cafes and bars, which can often help you out. Occasionally, *dortoirs* (attics or outbuildings attached to hotels) can be found – ask at hotels – and enterprising farmers sometimes convert barns for overnight use by walkers. The existence of hotels, inns, cafes and bars is mentioned in this guide wherever they occur, to the best of the author's knowledge at the time of going to press.

# Camping

Many towns and villages along GR5 are near a campsite (*terrain de camping*) or possess their own. Some are holiday centres in their own right with bars, restaurant, sports facilities and swimming pool (like one at Samoëns) and are heavily subscribed by continental family groups. Others cater for lightweight campers only, offering basic though adequate facilities.

Size and quality vary, as do prices. Some are privately owned, others municipally, others still are unofficial and without amenities but tacitly approved. Officially established sites are star-graded, like hotels, and prices displayed at reception. A backpacker or two with a small tent can almost always be squeezed into the busiest of sites and will rarely be asked to even produce a camping Carnet (proof of identity and third-party insurance). However, larger groups might have difficulty in popular areas in mid-season. (Carnets can be obtained from such organisations as the Camping Club of Great Britain, Youth Hostels Association, etc.) One of the very few perks (in the author's opinion) of an organised campsite is the opportunity it provides to shower and catch up on washing clothes and other chores. Evenings and nights can be noisy with the activity of holidaymakers who have less need of sleep than the walker at the end of a strenuous day! Farm pitching (*camping à la ferme*) is a more peaceful alternative and is spreading in popularity. If your French is up to it, do not hesitate to ask – country folk are friendly and will rarely refuse to help you.

Wild camping (*camping sauvage*) is possible in many places along GR5 but must always be subject to the following qualifications. Pitch well away from habitations unless you have asked for permission to camp, and preferably an hour or so's hike up from a road or *gîte*. Take care not to pollute water sources or foul the environment in any way –

the backpacker's code is to leave no sign of an overnight stay. If there is a high fire risk (e.g. in forest or scrub) **never** light an open fire and take special care with matches and cigarette ends. Take litter with you.

In the Vanoise National Park, camping is specifically forbidden and there are restrictions in other regions too. National Park wardens can impose a hefty fine for contravention of the ' no camping' rule. Some refuges now allow camping in their vicinity on payment of a small charge.

Wherever campsites and possibilities for farm and wild pitching exist along the trail, they are mentioned in the route guide, as are areas where camping is not allowed, to the best of the author's knowledge.

## Maps and Waymarking

The detailed route guide contained in this book will steer you adequately, and it is hoped enjoyably, down the narrow strip of the GR5 Traverse of the French Alps from Lac Léman (Lake Geneva) to Nice. Reference is made, where appropriate, to features and amenities off the trail to paint a broader picture of the regions and their walking possibilities, including official variants. Despite this, you will need to carry maps for three important reasons. First, as an essential navigational aid in mist or if the trail is lost. Second, to allow you to choose alternative or escape routes should bad weather or sickness/injury occur unexpectedly. Third, to help you identify features in the mountain landscape – peaks, rivers, glaciers, valleys, settlements, etc.

Eastern France and the Alps are well mapped by Edition Didier et Richard of Grenoble (where they have a superb shop). Their 1:50,000 maps, called 'Itineraires Pédestres et à Ski' (Hiking and skiing routes) cover GR5 and its variants and, because each sheet (with one exception) spans a large section of trail, they are good value and convenient to use. Sheet numbers required, north to south, are: 3, 8, 11, 6, 10, 1 & 9. The maps are overprinted to show clearly the location of refuges and *gîtes d'étapes*, as well as GR5 and other hiking trails (blue lines) and mountain ski routes (red lines). A word of caution – the blue hiking trail line is drawn at times rather crudely and in some places is inaccurate. The notes in this guide are based on the officially waymarked route at the time of going to press and should be followed in preference to the map markings if different.

Maps covering the GR5 are also produced by IGN (Institut

Géographique National) – the French equivalent to our Ordnance Survey – but you will need more of them. 1:50,000 sheets required, north to south, are: Thonon–Châtel; Samoëns–Pas dé Morgins; Cluses; Chamonix; St. Gervais-les-Bains; Bourg-Saint-Maurice; Modane; Névache; Briançon; Guillestre; Embrun; Aiguille de Chambeyron; Larche; St. Etienne-de-Tinée; Puget–Theniers; Le Boréon (for GR52); St. Martin–Vesubie; Menton & Nice.

Three IGN 1:25,000 'Cartes Touristiques' sheets are highly recommended for the Landry to Modane section through the Vanoise National Park, whichever variant you choose to follow. They are: 235 Tarentaise; 236 Grande Casse–Dent Parachée; 237 Haute-Maurienne. The detail quality is excellent and the trail accurately overprinted in red. Similar sheets on this scale called 'Cartes Topographiques' are invaluable for mountain exploration and winter hiking. Sheets show magnetic variations, as on British maps, 5° being average.

Finally, an IGN 1:1,000,000 map is available containing all GR routes in France and the location of the National Parks – an ideal sheet for planning routes and placing GR5 in the context of the network of long-distance trails as a whole.

For maps and guides, contact your local outdoor or book shop, which can order for you. Many of the sheets required can usually be bought from stock at Stanfords Ltd., 12 Long Acre, London WC2. Obviously French bookshops sell them too! Additional information on walking routes in the French Alps can be obtained from the French Government Tourist Office, 178 Piccadilly, London W1 or (in French) from the main organisation working on behalf of walkers in France – Fédération Française de la Randonnée Pédestre, 14 rue Riquet, 75019 PARIS; and from CIMES (Centre Informations Montagne et Sentiers), Maison du Tourisme, 14 Rue de la République, GRENOBLE (Isère), which also publishes a comprehensive guide to *gîtes* and refuges called *La Grande Traversée des Alpes*, in French.

GR routes are waymarked (*balisée*) using horizontal red and white painted stripes which appear on walls, trees, rocks, etc. along the trail. White above red signifies you are on the route; when doubled, and sometimes including an arrow, it means a change of direction is imminent; red and white stripes forming a cross means that the trail does not go that way. From time to time there are local variations on these themes but they are usually clear and easy to follow. Unfortunately, waymarks have a habit of appearing with hypnotic and unnecessary frequency on straightforward stretches and suddenly disappearing at a path junction or town, just when they are needed most! Perhaps it should be borne in mind that snow will obscure some waymarks during the winter months, making duplication in summer conditions more understandable. In any event, reference to this guide will hopefully clarify the way ahead and save much frustration from casting laboriously about. Occasionally, a painted 'GR5' metal plate or wooden sign announces that you are on the trail or that an important junction has been reached.

Although in the less frequented regions waymarks are sometimes in need of a lick of paint, one has to concede that the voluntary groups who carry out the work do a good job. Changes to the route brought about by landslip, forestry work, new building development and land ownership disputes all have to be accommodated, which is why patience should be shown when diversions on the ground contradict map and guide.

Signs denoting path directions and destinations carry distance expressed in hours and minutes, rather than kilometres, and are based on a walking speed of about 4 km per hour (2½ mph). If this seems fast, it is because few French walkers use tents, preferring to stay in refuges, *gîtes d'étapes* or shelters, and carry lighter packs. Times in this guide are based on the steady pace of a laden back-packer. Interestingly, the author has found this pace often quicker on ascents but slower on descents than the 'official' times. The reader, however, will soon fix his or her own pace relative to the times shown and make the necessary adjustments when planning ahead.

## Amenities and Services

Although the walker new to France might well be mesmerised by differences in customs and appearances, the enduring impression one is left with after a week or two there is of the many similarities between our societies. A few notes pertaining to the walker's needs, however, might not go amiss.

The majority of French take their annual summer holiday between July 14th (Bastille Day) and the last week of August. Throughout this period, popular regions (e.g. Chamonix–Mont-Blanc and the Vanoise) receive their greatest influx of visitors and consequently overnight accommodation is at peak demand. During late June/early July and again during late August/early September, trails are more sparsely populated, refuges and *gîtes d'étape* open but not crowded and the weather more likely to be pleasantly fine.

August 15th (Assumption Day) is a national Bank Holiday (the French have more than we do!) and leads into the period of return home for many French holidaymakers.

Banks normally open from 9 am to noon and 2 to 4 pm weekdays and close either Saturdays (mainly large towns) or Mondays. On the day before Bank Holidays, however, they close early and sometimes remain closed the day after. Opening times vary from region to region and, since GR5 passes through relatively few towns of any size, the walker is strongly advised to make provision for carrying adequate cash. Travellers cheques are always a good stand-by, as are well-known credit and debit cards in payment for some goods and services.

Post Offices are generally open between 8 am and 6 pm weekdays (closed for lunch sometimes) and 8 am till noon Saturdays.

Telephone call-boxes have sprouted up in towns and villages over recent years and it is now possible to make local and international calls with very little fuss. To call the UK, dial 00 44 then the UK number minus the first 0 of the STD code. There are telephones in bars and cafes, too, and some Post Offices have telephone cubicles – you ask and pay for the call over the counter. Emergency numbers are: Fire 18, Police and Mountain Rescue 17, Medical Emergencies 15, Operator and Directory Enquiries 12.

Most shops have half-day closing, often Mondays, but some food shops (particularly bakers) open on Sunday mornings. Opening hours tend to be longer for food shops (e.g. 7 am–6.30 pm) and 9 am–6.30 or 7.30 pm for other shops, and they frequently close from noon till 2 pm or even later.

To buy meats, paté and sausage, look for a *charcuterie*; for groceries an *épicerie* or *alimentation*; for cakes, pastries and sweets a *pâtisserie*; and for bread a *boulangerie*. Traditional French bakers have adjusted to the wholemeal/bran revolution and in addition to the long, white crusty loaves (*baguettes* or *pain long*) you can usually buy wholemeal bread (*pain complet*), rye bread (*pain de seigle*) and bran bread (*pain de son*). Fruit and veg are plentiful and delicious, as are the many and varied cheeses and cooked meats. Fresh milk is not always available but the UHT and dried varieties are. Packet soups, biscuits, cake, chocolate and tinned foods are on sale much as in equivalent British shops.

Continental breakfast, should you buy one, may only yield bread, butter and coffee, yet the French revere other formal mealtimes and it is sometimes more difficult to get a casual snack, like egg and chips, than in Britain. Even the humble but life-giving cuppa may be served weak, with hot milk and at an exorbitant price – you have been warned! If you do not wish to stop for a leisurely meal (often excellent value), pizzas are a satisfying alternative and, perhaps because Italy is never far away from GR5, seem to be widely available.

At hotels or campsites, you might be asked to complete a visitor registration form, giving details of your passport, length of stay, etc. This is a routine police formality.

Finally, French summertime is one hour ahead of British summertime (and thus two hours ahead of GMT).

Details of all services and amenities along GR5 and its environs appear in this book – see the key immediately preceding the Introduction.

## Clothing and Equipment

Many of the conditions found on British mountains in summer can be encountered in the French Alps, though on the whole the weather is warmer and rather less changeable than ours. (See section on 'Weather'). The further south you travel, the more generally settled and hotter it becomes and gear requirements will change accordingly. Weather is not wholly predictable, however, and when variations occur they can be dramatic – it is worth remembering that the GR5 trail often follows high paths through rugged and sometimes remote terrain. Good quality gear suitable for summer mountain walking in Britain can be confidently used during the same season on the routes covered by this book, but the following notes are relevant.

Whatever combinations of garments you prefer to use, they do need to be versatile in order to cope with potentially large differences in temperature and weather type. Multiple thin layers are more useful.

Shell clothing in the form of cagoule and overtrousers is a necessary insurance against wind and rain and, if made from a breathable, windproof material, can double as an insulating layer and reduce the total amount of clothing carried. Jeans should be avoided for serious walking as they offer little protection when wet and are usually too tight a fit.

Spare dry clothing, whilst adding weight to the rucsac, is well-nigh essential and good to change into after a damp day (rain or perspiration!) and for use in situations where personal freshness is desirable!

Shirts and underwear made from a quick-drying fabric like polyester cotton can be washed out with a little soap (biodegradable?) and hung off the sac, though socks and towels can be rather slow to dry. In good weather, items can readily be washed along the trail or at overnight halts – remembering, however, that detergent damages stream and pond life. A swimming costume can be worth its weight in gold if you hit a heat wave and, if you don't, will double as underwear.

Shorts will almost certainly be required, as will a brimmed sunhat (better than a peaked cap as it will shade the back of the neck and ears too). Good quality sunglasses protect the eyes from dazzling pale-coloured rock and snow, and a high-factor suncream will protect skin exposed to strong ultra-violet radiation in the thinner, clearer air at altitude. Take precautions to avoid sunburn just as you would on a beach holiday if your skin is sensitive.

Boots, traditional or lightweight, should be comfortably 'worn-in' rather than 'worn-out'. Good tread-depth reduces foot soreness through the sole and provides a more secure grip when traversing snowfields and steep slopes. One trek down GR5 virtually wore away the tread pattern on a new pair of reputable lightweight boots belonging to the author – witness to the rugged nature of much of the trail.

By the beginning of July, paths are usually free of snow except for the highest stretches, but very early in the season (mid-June, say) crampons and ice-axe might well be necessary safeguards on high, north-facing slopes. Amounts of snow differ from year to year, depending upon the severity or lateness of the preceding winter. Crossing the Col du Bonhomme towards the end of July, the author was surprised to hear that only three weeks previously much of the Tour du Mont Blanc had been heavily snowed up and impassable in many places to the ordinary trekker. If you are planning to walk before the beginning of July or after the end of September, it is advisable to enquire in advance about snow conditions before setting off to cross high passes.

Unless you are planning excursions onto glaciers or more difficult terrain, you will not need a rope – despite a few steep and exposed sections, GR5 and its variants are walking routes. Snow and boggy ground in mid-season are seldom a problem so full gaiters are not really necessary. The author finds elasticated anklets useful in preventing small stones, dust and even hopping insects from entering socks or boots.

Trainers or moccasins provide a welcome change of footwear when travelling or pottering around towns and villages; they are obligatory if you intend using refuges, *gîtes d'étape* or hotels. (See section on 'Accommodation'.)

Dairy herds brought up to the high mountain pastures for summer grazing frequent much of the northern half of GR5 and add their quota of insects to the indigenous population. Clegs (horseflies) seem to be the main pest but are deterred from biting by thorough applications of a good insect repellent.

Overnight halts above 2000 metres (about 6500 feet), particularly in a tent, can be decidedly chilly even in mid-summer, and frost is not uncommon above 2500 metres (8000 feet). If frequent high-level camping is anticipated, a 3-season sleeping bag and closed-cell foam bed mat are recommended. Alternatively, fleece underwear could be worn in a 2-season bag and posted home with other warm items if trekking down into the southern sector. 30% of the body's heat escapes via the head and a lightweight woolly hat keeps you cosy in chilly situations – at dawn or dusk, in mist or bad weather, on a cold night. In the Alpes-Maritimes, on the other hand, the main protection needed is likely to be against hot sunshine and thorny undergrowth.

A small torch is essential in a tent or refuge/*gîte* at night (especially if the latter is crowded with bodies!). It gets dark earlier in more southerly latitudes, particularly noticeable late in the season, and often mountains will block out daylight before sunset and after sunrise. Spare batteries and bulbs are best carried for emergencies.

Since chemist shops and doctors are thin on the ground in some regions, a comprehensive first-aid kit is advisable. As on British mountains, a whistle (see section on 'Mountain Safety') will increase your chances of being found if you are involved in an emergency (your own or someone else's). Use it only as a last resort as rescue costs are very high and will have to be paid once an operation is mounted, whether you actually need rescuing or not!

It is generally unnecessary to carry much drinking water as most high streams and springs are safe sources, subject to the usual common sense – if in doubt add sterilising tablets or boil. Many farms, hamlets and villages have troughs of crystal clear water fed from springs or brooks. It is vitally important in hot weather to regularly replace body fluid lost by sweating, so a water bottle of some kind is clearly essential. The author finds the 1½ litre plastic bottles in which mineral water is sold (a good safe drink!) to be lightweight, capacious and cheap to replace. Rigid, screw-top varieties might be preferred, however, while collapsible containers, with their greater capacity and versatility, are useful when camping. Along sections of the trail where no water sources exist, it is useful to know your fluid requirements and match bottle capacity accordingly.

A small French–English dictionary will take the guesswork from deciphering signs of all kinds if your knowledge of the language is poor or non-existent. Phrasebooks can be useful but tend not to cater for the mountain walker all that well.

Whether or not to carry a stove will depend upon your style of travel although, whilst brewing-up is a common delight to all walkers in temperate conditions, backpackers have the greatest need for a stove.

Methylated spirit (*acool à brûler*), is sold in most general provision shops and is much cheaper than in England. The French use this to prime their gas cookers. Petrol (*essence C*) is available from hardware shops and garages. Camping Gaz would seem to be the simplest fuel for a summer expedition and the familiar blue cartridges are widely available. (Not to be carried on aircraft.)

Stout plastic bags are invaluable damp-proofing for rucsac contents in rainy weather. Clothing, food, documents, film, etc. can be packed together, safely separated. Maps, guidebook and compass will need to be carried (see section on 'Maps and Waymarking') and a map case will earn its keep, as well on a wet day in the Alps as anywhere else!

Finally, ensure your clothing and gear are in good condition and try to keep the total weight down to what you are accustomed to carrying – gradients in the Alps are often steeper and ascents/descents longer than in Britain so every extra pound counts! You will enjoy the walking all the more for being reasonably fit – indeed, fitness and some previous mountain-walking experience are prerequisites on some sections of GR5. A programme of exercise in the month or two before departure is advisable if you do not already walk in the hills or exercise regularly. Cycling, jogging, walking with a loaded rucsac and even swimming will all build stamina and increase heart/lung efficiency.

## Mountain Safety

The international distress call is a series of six visual or audible signals per minute, followed by a minute's pause and then repeated (see box inside front and back covers). The reply is three such signals per minute with a minute's pause before repeating. The distress signal can be given in whichever way seems most appropriate to attract attention – blowing a whistle, shouting, flashing a torch at night, or the sun in a mirror by day, etc.

Another generally recognised signal, especially from the air, is to raise both arms straight up, meaning 'I need help', or raising one arm only, meaning 'I do not need help'.

Whilst not wishing to over dramatise, the author feels obliged to remind would-be trekkers on GR5 of the potentially serious nature of many of its higher stretches. However, walkers who are properly equipped and provisioned, experienced in the use of map and compass and accident/injury procedures, fit enough to cover the planned day's route without becoming exhausted and who have up-to-date weather information should have no trouble on even the most remote and rugged sections.

Not all parts of the French Alps are popular with walkers and in some areas you may encounter few people, making self-reliance an important attribute if things go wrong. If in doubt, wait for conditions to improve or turn back. Mountain rescue can be summoned by dialling 17 on the nearest telephone.

It should be said that the majority of hikers on GR5 enjoy an invigorating and memorable trek with merely the usual rash of minor mishaps and discomforts to contend with. Generally, only those who are careless or ill-prepared come to grief.

Holiday insurance policies will usually cover walking in the Alps provided you do not use specialist climbing or winter sports-type equipment like ropes, pitons, crampons, ice-axe or skis. But check the small print first! You will probably also be eligible for medical cover in France using form E111, available from your local Social Security office or Post Office.

# Weather

The Northern and Southern Alps are separated geographically and climatologically by a line roughly linking the southern boundaries of the Vanoise, Ecrins and Vercors National Parks. The Savoie and Dauphiné regions of the Northern Alps are characterised by a moist, cool and temperate climate, luxuriant vegetation and plentiful water in summer from melting snow. Because of the severity and length of winters, however, permanent human settlement is possible only at relatively low altitudes and in sheltered valleys.

The south Dauphiné, Briançonnais, Queyras, Ubaye, Alpes-de-Haute-Provence and Alpes-Maritimes regions, on the other hand, are much drier and the Mediterranean climate allows the inhabitants to live at altitudes that would be unthinkable in the north. St.-Veran, for instance, is the highest village in Europe at 2040 metres (6693 ft).

During the summer, the Alps are generally well away from the main areas of weather disturbance travelling east across the Atlantic, so that a weak atmospheric circulation prevails. Wind speeds at high altitudes are generally low, weather situations slow to change, with vertical air movement due to thermal exchanges often more pronounced than horizontal movements of the air masses.

Disturbed weather does occur from time to time, however, despite the more settled overall pattern and it is useful for the walker or climber to be able to recognise changes and be prepared to plan accordingly. There are three main types of disturbed summer weather:

## 1. The cycle of approximately ten days

During June, July and August, and more rarely in September, a cycle is set up in the development of atmospheric conditions. Immediately after a temporary worsening of the weather (which will be mentioned later) a slow improvement takes place over forty-eight hours or so. Showers become infrequent, winds are mainly from the northern sector, air temperature is low for the season and visibility excellent. From the third day onwards, this fine weather becomes established; skies are generally clear and the temperature rises day by day, high altitude winds weakening all the time and veering towards the south-east. Any clouds are only over summits and disappear at the end of the afternoon, followed by a clear night. The weather appears to be set fair and unchanging and yet each day the air temperature gets higher and winds at altitude are more and more southerly in direction. Around the eighth or ninth day, the end of the cycle will be approaching. Winds at high altitude strengthen from the south-west and the sky becomes cloudy in a very short time, with heavy cumulo-nimbus clouds giving storms. The abundance and density of the clouds make progress of any kind in the mountains difficult, if not dangerous, with thick mist down to 1500 metres, violent showers and gusts of wind in the squalls often intensified by the topography. The air temperature can drop five to ten degrees Centigrade in as many minutes, adding to the dangers for the walker or climber caught up high in the mountains. It is rare, however, for such bad conditions to last for more than a few hours, although clouds can build again after a temporary lull when winds have veered to a more north-westerly quarter.

## 2. A daily weather cycle

This pattern of weather disturbance can recur on several consecutive days, unfolding over each twenty-four hour period in the following way.

At dawn there is no wind, air temperature is slightly higher than normal and the sky is partly cloudy with excellent visibility. During the morning, subtle changes take place as clouds form themselves into 'cells' and grow heavier. From midday onwards, summits over 2000 metres are obscured. Since high altitude winds are very weak, clouds concentrate over the higher massifs, becoming taller and heavier during the afternoon until suddenly the storms burst, often accompanied by thunder and lightning. This type of weather pattern is due to instability in the air layers of the lower atmosphere and the thermal effects of the sun's heat.

## 3. The almost stationary front

This feature is an exception rather than the rule but in certain years can be frequently encountered. It is characterised by a cloudy sky, often with a ceiling at 3000–5000m. It rains irregularly, at any time of day, but is not windy even at high altitude. For the walker/climber it is a typically wet, depressing summer! The pattern often changes only very slowly so the dull, damp conditions last for periods of several days at a time.

Whilst the reader walking GR5 may recognise one or more of these weather types, it is always possible that he or she will experience an atypical episode, the more so if the trek is an extended one. The author has been desiccated by hot winds blowing up from Africa in the Northern Alps, plagued for days by the subsequent thunderstorms and only narrowly missing tornadoes near Nice which devastated parts of the coastal plain – all within the space of four weeks!

As in Britain, it is always advisable to keep a weather eye open and to obtain a forecast before travelling into high and exposed terrain. Thunderstorms can develop rapidly in the mountain regions and are sometimes extremely violent. In the section between St. Dalmas-Valdeblore and Trois-Communes on the GR52 variant, for example, summer storms are notorious and must be taken seriously as an objective risk. If a thunderstorm is imminent, avoid the following places if you can: summits and ridges (lightning can be observed travelling **along** ridges!); cliff edges or by high cairns; near splits or cracks in the mountain or in caves; next to streams or beneath a cliff; close to the shore of a lake; underneath isolated trees; close to metal objects, groups of animals or people. Safe places to be include: amongst trees lower than the average tree height in the surrounding area; in a depression at least twice as deep as the tallest nearby object; 15 to 25 metres (50 to 80 feet) from the face of a cliff; below and between flat boulders. If you are caught out on open ground, kneel with hands on knees, head well down, preferably on an insulating layer of rucsac, rope coil, etc. The theory is that a lightning strike will earth itself via your arms and knees rather than via your head and heart. The author hopes you will never have to put it to the test!

Weather forecasts can be obtained in several ways. Local or regional newspapers usually carry a 'Meteo', with weather map and synopsis (your French–English dictionary will help). Telephone directories give the number of Meteorological Offices and some, like Chamonix, can usually be prevailed upon to give you a forecast in English. There are also numbers for pre-recorded bulletins, for those whose French is up to it! Airports such as Modane and Nice will furnish up-to-the-minute weather information and the author has found them willing to try a little English – usually enough to get the gist! Local Syndicates d'Initiative or Maisons du Tourisme (Tourist Information Centres) often post up the current forecast or will give you details on request. Finally, weather information can usually be obtained from refuges, *gîtes* and hotels in mountain areas.

# Flora and Fauna

One can divide vegetation into zones occurring at different altitudes. However, these zones are not always distinct, instead merging gradually and being affected by height, exposure to sun and wind, the underlying rock type and latitude. Many species are found at greater altitudes the further south one travels.

In the sub-alpine zone, below the upper limits of forest, numerous varieties of lowland and mountain species exist together. Most of the common flowers of the British Isles can be found in this zone, along with those native only to the Alps. Plants at this level range from small to very large, being more plentiful and varied than those in the true alpine zones above 2300m (7500ft).

Travelling upwards, you will pass through luxuriant meadows of flowers and through shady forests. In the meadows you are sure to see the magnificent spires of the Great Yellow Gentian and the rich bells of the Purple Gentian. If you are fortunate, you may spot a solitary Martagon Lily or one of the many different orchids.

At the upper tree-line, plants such as juniper, birch and alder become stunted and sparse, eventually giving way to true alpine plants. Here the flora is more limited and highly specialised. Dwarf shrubs such as evergreen Alpenrose, with its pinkish, bell-shaped flowers, thrive up to 2800m (9000ft). Other flowers living in these high pastures are the gaily coloured purple and yellow Alpine Aster and the large blue Trumpet Gentian.

Higher still, the meadows thin and give way to rocky and apparently barren slopes above 2800m (9000ft), but even here brightly coloured flowers thrive in clefts and cracks. Amongst these gems of high mountain places are the bright pink 'flower-cushions' of Rock Jasmine, the delicate, wavering purple heads of the Alpine Pansy and the bright blue stars of the Spring Gentian. Growing right on the very edge of the snow-line is the shapely and delicate purple Alpine Snowbell.

Further south, especially in the Alpes-Maritimes, where spring is earlier, plants are more resistant to drought conditions. Amongst these are numerous varieties of Stonecrop, Carline Thistle and the brilliant flowers of the Painted Pink.

Sadly, picking wild flowers, even rare species, is still commonplace in France and it is not unusual to see families descending in the afternoon clutching huge bunches of them! The result is that many flowers, including the once common Edelweiss, are becoming hard to find. With an increase in the number of walkers enjoying the alpine environment, conservation of the natural habitat is the responsibility of us all. A good close-up photograph of a specimen is, after all, a more considerate and enduring response than taking it away altogether. If the weight can be accommodated, a small alpine flower book is a useful 'extra', enabling you to identify some of the many and varied species which border so much of the trail.

There are, of course, numerous species of birds, mammals and insects living in the diverse habitats of alpine snow and rock and in the lush, vegetated river valleys. Many of the species are found in Britain too, but for the mountain walker in the French Alps, there are three creatures whose presence seems to epitomise high, wild country and sightings of which are especially rewarding.

First, and by far the most common, is the marmot, whose piercing, wolf-whistle warning cry becomes a familiar sound on grassy and stony mountainsides up to about 2700m (8800ft). Although there are some 13 species worldwide, it is found in its original habitat only in the Alps and High Tatras. Living gregariously, each individual weighs about 5–6kg and eats plant greenery. Burrows reach down 3 metres (and as much as 10 metres in length), with several exits, and here marmots hibernate from around October to April, living off body fat. In late May or early June, females give birth to between two and six naked and blind young; thanks to strict protection, population levels are rising.

Perhaps the second most likely high-mountain mammal to be sighted is the chamois, though fewer numbers and greater shyness make them more elusive. Look for them on barely accessible rocky slopes, over which they move with uncanny sure-footedness, up to around the 4000m (13,000ft) level. Chamois live in groups of between fifteen and thirty individuals, though old males are often solitary.

The mountain ibex (bouqetin) inhabits the whole Alpine range and can be seen at altitudes over 3500m (11,500ft). Its original home also includes the mountains of north-east Sudan, eastern Egypt and the Arabian peninsula. Females are substantially smaller than males and their horns are shorter and more slender. Old bucks can weigh up to 80kg, with horns exceeding one metre in length.

# Photography

*Cameras, lenses and filters* – Pocket cameras are ideally suited to snap-shot photography where the subject is at fairly close range, but their technical limitations often produce disappointing results when used to record mountain scenery. If your photographic intentions are more serious, you are likely to take along a 35mm single lens reflex camera with some accessories and it is hoped the following notes will be of some practical help.

The standard 50mm lens will produce rather too narrow a field of view for the expansive landscape of the French Alps, although for many general subjects on the trail it performs well. A wide-angle lens is strongly recommended.

Including a medium telephoto allows you to 'pull in' summits, ridges, villages, people and wild-life and to isolate close-up subjects by using a shallow depth of field. In the usually brilliant light of the French Alps, a teleconverter (which reduces the maximum available aperture by several stops) can be used successfully to produce a tele-photo effect without the bulk and weight of a telephoto lens.

Zooms, whilst heavier than prime lenses, offer a popular compromise and remove the necessity to change lenses – not always a convenient operation in bad weather or on steep ground. There is, of course, a weight penalty involved in carrying extra photographic equipment but superior results will always justify this to the enthusiast, providing a rich and vivid record of experiences.

Camera and lenses need protection at all times from moisture, dust, heat and impact – the very elements encountered every day on the trail! Padded pouches are commercially available which attach to the rucsac hip-belt or can be tucked inside a rucsac pocket. A puffer-brush and lens cleaning tissues are to your camera what a toilet kit is to you – the means to stay reasonably clean!

An ultra-violet or skylight filter is essential at altitude to reduce the haze effect of UV light and to correct the blue bias it produces on colour film. The filter, left in place, also usefully protects the front lens element against accidental damage. A polarizing filter will significantly reduce reflections in glass and on water surfaces and when used with colour film will darken blue sky and generally increase colour saturation.

*Looking south across the Alpes-Maritimes from the Pas de la Cavale*

*Film and exposure* – A speed rating in the approximate range 50–200 ASA will adequately cover most subjects. Colour slides produce more accurate images than prints but need to be projected for optimum viewing effect. Moreover, correct exposure is of prime importance when using slide film as differences of only half a stop can be critical to faithful colour reproduction. Use of an incident light meter will help, but if in doubt 'bracketing' is the safest solution. Take one shot at the estimated correct exposure, one at a half-stop more exposure and one a half-stop less. Undeniably you use more film, but bracketing greatly increases the chance of coming home with successful pictures (many of which will be unrepeatable).

Colour prints are more immediately accessible for viewing than slides and minor exposure errors can be compensated for in the laboratory – good reason why many prefer their photography in this form.

Whichever film type is used, it is worth bearing in mind that when photographing at high altitude where snow and rock reflect back large amounts of light, and particularly during the middle hours of the day when the sun is brilliant, exposure mistakes can and do occur, however careful the photographer is. Simple cameras may be fooled into under-exposing in such bright lighting conditions, producing disappointingly dark pictures.

Heat is film's number one enemy and will significantly degrade the quality of the processed image. Colour film is especially vulnerable and must be protected from prolonged exposure to hot sunshine. Unused and exposed film stock can be packed deep in the centre of the rucsac, surrounded by other insulating items like foam mat, clothing, etc. And don't forget the film already loaded in your camera – try to carry it on the shady side of your body.

Although exposed film is best processed promptly, there is a risk from X-ray damage if it is posted back to Britain, particularly if the packaging is other than the recognisable manufacturer's envelope.

Well-known film types and sizes are widely available in France, but away from population centres choice is very limited and storage conditions suspect. Better to take with you what you think you will need.

## Key to the Route Guide

For the purpose of this guide, the GR5 Grande Traversée des Alpes has been divided into six stages, each representing around five days' walking and finishing at a strategic valley:

- Lac Léman to les Houches (Chamonix valley)
- Les Houches to Landry (Isère valley)
- Landry to Modane (3 variants through the Vaniose National Park)
- Modane to Ceillac (near the Guil valley)
- Ceillac to St. Etienne-de-Tinée to Nice.

Since walkers vary widely as to pace and individual objectives, and have different requirements for overnight accommodation, the author has refrained from laying out the Route Guide in day sections, which might suit some but not others. Instead, each important point along the trail (such as village, path junction, col, etc.) appears in heavier type, preceded by the time taken to reach it from the previous point. This is expressed in hours and minutes. Following each point on the trail is its height above sea level (in metres and feet) and what it offers the walker in the way of views, water, shelter, etc.; and in the

Les Dents Blanches – a short section in Switzerland, Stage 1

Aiguille de la Nova (centre top) from Col de Bresson, Stage 2

case of towns and villages, what supplies and services are available. Please note, however, that mention of bars, cafes, restaurants and hotels is no guarantee of quality (or even their existence!), which may vary from the rudimentary to the exclusive. Where the plural is used there may be just two, or a considerably greater number, of the establishments concerned.

The word 'provisions' indicates that only a limited range of goods is available, mainly food items. 'All supplies' means that you are likely to be able to obtain most commodities.

PTT (Postes, Téléphone & Télécommunications) denotes a post office (including telephone); SNCF (Societé National de Chemin de Fer) is a railway station.

Accurate when going to press, the locations, capacities, opening periods and facilities of each refuge and *gîte d'étape* on or near GR5 are included, as are bus services, where they occur. Campsites and suggestions for wild camping pitches appear in the text, along with notes of when services such as banks and tourist offices are available and where car parking space (often very limited) can be found.

It is thus possible for individual walkers, whatever their style of travel, to plan each day's hiking by adding up the route times from start to finishing points and by weighing up what possibilities lie ahead for obtaining food, drink and shelter.

Route directions are given for the south-bound walker and in the text are abbreviated thus: R = right; L = left. (The R and L banks of streams and rivers are given as they appear facing the GR5's direction of travel.)

Compass points are expressed as initial letters too, thus S = south, NW = north-west, etc.

Finally, the author wishes to point out that whilst every effort has been made to provide accurate and reliable information, changes to the trail and amenities do occur from time to time on such a long and complex route as GR5.

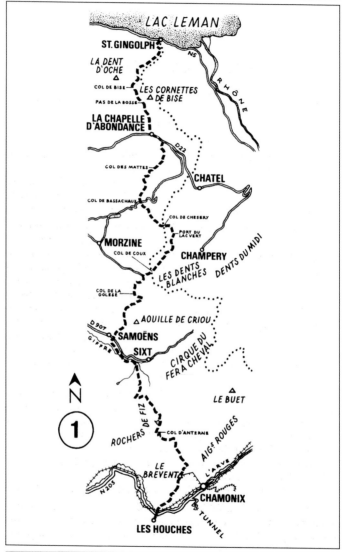

## STAGE ONE

# LAC LÉMAN TO THE CHAMONIX VALLEY

## 5–6 days

Lac Léman, fed by the upper Rhône and the Dranse, is largest of the Alpine lakes, and along its picturesque shores are strung the beaches and pleasure-boat harbours of spa resorts like Evian and Thonon, twin capitals of the Chablais. It is from here that the GR5 Grande Traversée des Alpes begins its long journey southward to the Mediterranean.

Our first stage crosses the northern Pre-alps of the Haute Savoie, a limestone mountain mass separating France from Switzerland and rising to the Dent d'Oche and Cornettes de Bise. At first, below the rocky summits, it is a green, picturesque landscape of high meadows thick with wild flowers and cool, deep forests; of ancient chalets and tantalising views ahead to snow-capped peaks. These grassy cols, of Bise, Mattes, Chésery, Coux and Golèse, though strenuous enough to climb, have a gentle, almost domestic quality and are never far from settlements. In the architecture of towns and villages lives a strong sense of history and tradition, despite their continuing development as year-round resorts. Above, on the high mountain pastures, brown and white Abondance dairy herds graze to the tune of their cowbells.

As the great barrier of the high-altitude Northern Alps is approached, the terrain becomes more rugged and remote. From Samoëns to the Chamonix valley, across the Anterne and Brévent cols, spectacular waterfalls and amphitheatres of rock introduce breath-taking panoramas of the Mont Blanc massif. For the first time, the walker enters a region of permanent snowfields, yet in season he is seldom alone as the trails are well frequented, and from the Col de Brévent GR5 joins together with the route of the Tour du Mont Blanc.

Since the 'William Tell' first steamed across Lac Léman back in 1823, boats large and small have regularly plied its waters and it still provides quite the most exhilarating approach to Saint-Gingolph,

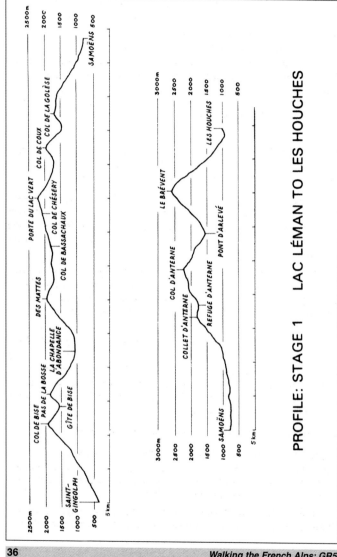

PROFILE: STAGE 1    LAC LÉMAN TO LES HOUCHES

nestling beneath the backdrop of the Dent d'Oche massif. The Compagnie Générale de Navigation operates a local ferry service, calling at Montreux around 10 am.

The GR5E variant has Thonon-les-Bains as its starting point and is a longer, more pastoral introduction, climbing gradually through the Thonon forest. After crossing the Dranses rivers at their confluence, the trail mounts steadily into the magnificent Dent d'Oche massif to join GR5 just below the Col de Bise. Route notes for this variant appear at the end of the chapter covering this section.

**SAINT-GINGOLPH** 386m (1266ft) – *all supplies, bars, cafes, restaurants, hotels, campsite, water, PTT, bank, bureau de change, doctor/pharmacy, buses for Evian and Thonon (SNCF).*

From the jetty, turn R along the waterfront, bedecked with flowers, then L up to the main street (N5). Turn R over the Franco-Swiss border and along past the PTT on the R. Turn L on D30 (Route de Novel), and just before passing under a bridge notice the very first GR5 waymark on a wall.

A junction is reached after 150 metres, at which proceed up Rue des Gaulles. In 100 metres, another junction – keep straight ahead, passing a shrine on the R, then gardens. Fork L after about 75 metres and walk up the lane which soon becomes a stony track – the ancient route to Novel.

Ignore paths off L and follow the old road up, mostly through pleasantly shady, deciduous woods with the deep ravine of the Morge torrent L, the border between France and Switzerland. There are several shrines by the wayside and, if you're lucky, wild strawberries. On reaching the D30, cross it and in 50 metres take a path R, behind a wall and past a small graveyard. The track leads up to

● 1h 30 m – **NOVEL** 960m (3150ft) – *hotels, restaurant.*

Turn L opposite two hotels and take the middle of three roads which winds up through this 700 year old village, once France's Gretna Green. Pass the telephone and the church, and at a bend note the path off R – a variant called the 'Tour du Léman'.

Look out for paths R which cut the road zig-zags. After the second short-cut, you pass a chapel and shrine and a stone statue of a deer. A short distance along D30 a waymark signals another short-cut, continuing as a rough path and reaching a wider track at a chalet. Take the path opposite which soon leads out across open pasture below chalets at

● 40m – **LA PLANCHE** 1160m (3806ft) – *D30 roadhead, car parking, water.*

Cross the road and turn L at a sign on a tree, over a clear stream following a well-waymarked path through conifer forest and out across tree-dotted meadows.

The path climbs steadily, in and out of forest, zig-zagging up flowery slopes to a spur L with sensational retrospective views. Ahead is the Ravin des Nez, one of the Morge's feeder streams, which is followed, level for a while, to the Chalets de Neuteu.

More steeply now, the trail climbs a small spur through drifts of wild flowers in early summer and with magnificent views back to Lac Léman. Ahead loom the rocky outliers of the Dent d'Oche and, to the L, the Tête de Charousse. Ignore a thin trod L and continue for a short distance to a large rock. This is the junction with the GR5E variant, coming up from Thonon-les-Bains.

GR5 makes a sharp L turn towards the Col de Bise (aptly named – Col of the North Wind), whose wooden cross is clearly visible in good weather. It is possible to take any of several rather indistinct trods here to link up with a clear path contouring the slopes ahead R. Avoid getting below a boulder slope L, although it is possible to rejoin the correct line further along.

Wild camping pitches abound beneath these final slopes and there are several springs. The path leads straightforwardly up to the

● 2h – **COL DE BISE** 1916m (6286ft) – *views NW to the Dent d'Oche and SE to les Cornettes de Bise; path L along ridge to Tête de Charousse and la Dent du Velon on the Franco-Swiss border.*

Ahead are magnificent views of the Cornettes de Bise and the snow-capped peaks in Switzerland beyond. The zig-zag descent threads down across green pastures, with spectacular cliff overhangs R. After crossing a stream, the trail approaches the

● 45m – **CHALETS DE BISE** 1506m (4941ft) – *bar (snacks), Refuge de Bise (70 places, guardian 16/6 to 30/9, bedding and cooking equip-*

*ment, toilet, restaurant service), water, car parking and road access from Vacheresse.*

The large herds of cows and goats are a feature of the valley and attract visitors to the little cluster of farm buildings around which the animals congregate, their bells ringing melodiously. Altogether a delightful spot, though the lake just below the roadhead is almost completely choked by weed. At its SW corner, however, are possibilities for discreet wild camping.

Pass the CAF refuge and large shed on a clear and increasingly stony path which climbs to

● 50m – **PAS DE LA BOSSE** 1815m (5955ft) – *path L for ascent of les Cornettes de Bise, 2432m (7979ft); path R, below col, for Ubine refuge (4h via Chalets de Mens and Col d'Ubine, with rock climbs on the 1200ft north face of Mt. Chauffé).*

*Church at la Chapelle-d'Abondance*

The view ahead over the Abondance valley is dominated by the jagged crest of the Dents du Midi and there is a glimpse, slightly L, of the distant Grande Combin. From the col, GR5 heads straight down the stone-strewn depression ahead, indistinctly but past waymarked rocks, to a muddy pond. (An alternative is to contour R past a ruined chalet before descending to the pond.) Thereafter, the path is clear, down to the Chalets de la Cheneau, and beyond follows the bottom of the shallow valley for 300 metres amidst a profusion of flowers and down through delightful pine forest to join a broad track from the Col de Vernez, L.

The Chalets de Chevenne are dotted hereabouts and there are wild camp pitches. At the road (parking space), turn L and head straight down to

● 1h 45m – **LA CHAPELLE D'ABONDANCE** – *all supplies, bars, restaurants, Gîte de la Chapelle d'Abondance (20 places, guardian 20/12 to 20/4 and 1/7 to 31/8, bedding), hotels, water, PTT, tourist information, buses for Abondance, Thonon and Châtel, taxi. N.B. – no more supplies until Samoëns.*

A prospering ski resort, la Chapelle's principal attraction in summer is its many beautiful timber chalets and barns, some very old. With their steep, snow-shedding roofs, balconies and wood stores, they possess an unpretentious, truth-to-materials quality lacking in so much modern architecture.

Route-finding on the next stretch to Lenlevay chalet, some five hours distant, is not all plain sailing, so directions are given in some detail. Follow waymarks wherever possible.

Turn L along D22, past numerous hotels and large modern chalets and in about 1 kilometre (¾ mile), having passed through the hamlet of Le Pantiaz, turn R by a concrete lamp standard just after a little bridge. Proceed down the lane, over the river, between two barns and across a field, whence the track enters a wood. Turn L, following a stream (signed 'Sur Bayard' and 'Route Forestière'). The waterfall R at a junction, and only 5 minutes away, is worth a visit. GR5 turns L, however, to reach an unmarked T-junction and into a broad track at a wooden barrier. Turn R and continue climbing in the forest to emerge at a waymarked boulder and signpost.

Sur Bayard chalet is just below L and the route hereabouts is confusing. A reasonable solution, in the author's experience, is to bear L alongside the wire fence on a good path, with superb retrospective views to the Pas de la Bosse and les Cornettes de Bise. Where the fence turns 90 degrees L, leave the good path (which leads back to the valley) and find an unconvincing path sharp R up through small trees and into a clearing. Follow the clearing's L edge then aim up for red and white waymarked trees and a rock. The path coming in from the R is GR5,

*Les Cornettes de Bise seen from the Abondance valley*

along which turn L and climb steadily through beautiful conifer forest on a clear but often muddy path.

At the Chalets des Crottes clearing, offering possible wild pitches, turn L. Climbing all the time now, the path eventually follows a stony stream bed up before bearing off R and emerging into open pasture at

● 1hr 45m – **LA TORRENS** 1742m (5715ft) – *dairy produce, water, shelter, camping possible.*

Pass the chalet's L corner and follow a sometimes indistinct trod in the general direction of the Col des Mattes on the skyline ahead R. Passing through low alders, the trail soon climbs more steeply up shaley, marshy ground by a stream to

● 1h – **COL DES MATTES** 1910m (6266ft).

In good conditions, a magnificent view awaits, from L to R – Dents du Midi, Dents Blanches and Mont Blanc itself peeping above in the far distance.

Head across grassy levels to the chalet ahead with its little pond, then bear half R on a small path descending gently. At a large waymarked rock turn sharp L across a pathless area and pick up the trail starting just below, contouring back across the same slope. Follow this down to Pron, visible below. Pass round the back of the chalets then drop straight down a steep grassy bank to a waymarked rock and on down to join a path at a fir tree. Turn R along this lumpy, boggy path and at a pretty waterfall R, drop down L to reach the broad track below. Turn R onto it, forking R immediately up past L'Etrye farm and on, first up zig-zags then gently down to

● 1h 30m – **LENLEVAY** 1745m (5725ft) – *water.*

Continue along the rough but level track for about 3 kilometres (under 2 miles), through thin conifer forest to a sharp L bend at a waymarked tree. Leave the track here, continuing over grass along the marshy path and finally climbing to the bar/restaurant building on the

● 1h 15m – **COL DE BASSACHAUX** 1783m (5850ft) – *bar/restaurant, car parking and road access from le Lindaret and Châtel. (30 min on road towards Châtel – Gîte de Plaine-Dranse, 19 places).*

The restaurant serves exquisite omelettes and *frites* (French fries)

*Looking towards Les Dent Blanches from Porte du Lac Vert*

and from your table you can see right back along the trail over the Dranse d'Abondance valley to the Col des Mattes.

GR5 turns L at the restaurant, along the wide level track contouring the SW slopes of the Tête de Lindaret, 1953m (6407ft). Ignore other tracks off L at a new ski development building, pass beneath a chair lift and continue until the track becomes a mountain path and climbs gently onto the vast, grassy expanse of

● 1h 35m – **COL DE CHÉSERY** 2025m (6644ft) – *Franco-Swiss border, wild camping possibilities.*

The little customs post ahead R has long since been closed but is still maintained. Once the big snowdrifts have cleared from the motorable track over to the Champéry valley (the only route out for dairy produce) cows are brought up for grazing and are milked at the cluster of sheds near the NW corner of the turquoise Lac Vert. There is also a resident flock of sheep.

Cross an area of hummocks and rocky outcrops on one of several paths, arriving at the recently built

● 10m – **REFUGE DE CHÉSERY** *(35 places, guardian during summer months, light meals and drinks; sells fishing permits for Lac Vert).*

To the NW are the impressive cliffs of Pointe de Chésery, Cornebois and Tête du Géant beneath the frontier ridge. On a hot, still afternoon you can hear the hollow rattle of rockfalls set off by the sun's warmth.

The track passes round the east side of the lake and leads up to

● 50m – **PORTE DU LAC VERT** 2157m (7077ft).

The panorama ahead is breathtakingly beautiful and one of the highlights of this stage. Across the upper Champéry valley is ranged a high mountain barrier, L to R – Dents du Midi, 3260m (10,695ft); Grand-Mont-Ruan, 3035m (9957ft); les Dents Blanches, 2727m (8947ft) and the Tête de Bossetan, 2406m (7894ft).

This section in Switzerland, to the SE of the frontier ridge formed by the Pointes of Chavanette, Fornet, Léchère and le Vanet, was inaugurated to replace the original GR5 routing via Le Lindaret, which is now a popular surfaced motor road.

Leave the Porte du Lac Vert L, turning R at a signed junction and descending gradually to a small bar (will take French francs!). Fork R past the next chalet, contouring along under a chair-lift. Join a motorable track round the head of the side valley, past a small chair-lift station. At Pisaz farm (camping possible), pass through a metal gate then aim for the L corner of buildings and a descending track, with the Col de Coux's little customs house clear ahead. Continue to

● 1h 30m – **POYA** 1653m (5423ft) – *water.*

The chalet is cunningly built into a rock overhang. Soon you join the track coming up from Champéry which mounts, beautifully graded all the way and flanked by rhododendrons, to the

● 45m – **COL DE COUX** 1925m (6315ft) – *Franco-Swiss border; path L to summit of La Berte, 1993m (6539ft), 15 mins.*

An accessible little col, with signposts and wide views. Leave it L, down through alders and along a small spur with the spectacularly folded cliffs of Les Terres Maudites L. The path drops into pine forest, and leads straight downhill onto a delightful zig-zag path.

*(30 min R, at le Pas, Chalet de Mines-d'Or, restaurant and rooms.)*

Turning L, the track winds pleasantly down through mature forest to the roadhead from Morzine. Water and car parking space.

Take a stony track L, over a stream and through alder and silver birch, before dropping down half-L to cross bouldery pasture with occasional waymarked rocks. Ignore a thin path R and pass through a shady copse by a large conspicuous rock outcrop. The narrow, stony path continues round the head of the Morzine valley, through profuse wild flowers, with chalets below and cattle grazing. Turn L onto a broader track which becomes a path again, winding attractively in and out of trees.

*Common Columbine*

*Trumpet Gentian*

*(Note: the path above the Chardonniére chalets is almost impossible to find. Waymarks now lead down to the chalet which is a gîte with bar and restaurant. From the gîte cross the river by the bridge and take a very steep forest road to the Col de la Golèse.)*

At a path junction, turn L and climb to the

● 2h – **COL DE LA GOLÈSE** 1659m (5443ft) – *water*.

This narrow passage beneath the rocky escarpment of the Pointe de la Golèse is an important migratory route for birds and insects.

Ornithologists have drawn interesting conclusions about the cyclical nature of certain flight-paths. Coal-tits, for example, pass through Golèse every other year, en route for Italy, Spain and even Egypt, whereas blue-tits use the col every year – one was caught seven years in a row! Other researchers are studying the passage of migratory insects like mosquitoes and bluebottles.

At the author's last visit the col also bore a word of significance for the southbound long-distance human migrator – 'Nice', scrawled in red paint on a rock!

Continue ahead on a good track into the Giffre valley, and on reaching the Chavonnes chalets bear SE then E to pass the Bervalles chalets. Soon GR5 joins the GR de Pays and continues SW to

● 45m – **CHALETS DE BOSSETAN** 1602m (5256ft) – *water, shelter.*

Descend the very stony track, in and out of forest, for what may seem an eternity (be thankful you're not climbing up it!), to reach a minor road (car parking space). Turn L and follow it down to

● 1h – **LES ALLEMANDS** 1028m (3373ft) – *food, water, road access from Samoëns. Gîte Couve-Loup, 29 places, meals.*

The road passes through the hamlet with its delightful ancient chalets after which you short-cut three long zig-zags. Having lost so much height (950m, over 3000ft), the Aouille de Criou towers overhead with almost unbelievable verticality, dominating the approach to Samoëns.

Follow the road down to a small reservoir then turn off L (SE) through forest to reach a footbridge. Do not cross but keep R, parallel to the Clèvieux torrent on a ski piste. This rejoins the road at Les Fontaines, where there are lovely crystal-clear shallows and pools to drink from or cool off in. Walk on down the road, past modern chalets and downhill to

● 1h 15m – **MOULINS** 730m (2395ft) – *water, access to Samoëns.*

So-called because of the numerous water mills (*moulins*) used to generate power for the hamlet at one time. Ice-cold water from the Dents Blanches massif up to the NE runs down in fast-moving channels alongside the road.

The long descent from the Col de la Golèse can be especially arduous on a hot day, with the afternoon sun dead ahead and the valley heat an unwelcome contrast to the cooler air of the previous higher-level walking. At a signpost 'Sixt-fer-a-Cheval', turn R for

● 10m – **SAMOËNS** 700m (2296ft) – *all supplies, bars, cafes, restaurants, hotels, campsite (with swimming pool!), water, PTT, bank, tourist information, doctor/pharmacy, buses for Anne-masse and for Cluses (SNCF), taxi, mountain rescue, Wednesday market, Alpine Garden.*

Samoëns has grown around a lime tree, now 500 years old, and its population, once decimated by epidemics and emigration, is only a third of its level in the 14th century. However, even that is changing as the Giffre valley continues to grow in popularity as a winter sports and summer holiday destination. It is famous for its stonemasons who, over the last three centuries, have built such structures as the quay at Rochefort-sur-Mer, the Saint-Quentin canal, the citadels of Besançon and Grenoble and the Ecluse fort.

Exit the town on D907, turning R along the bank of the Clèvieux to where it joins the Giffre at an area of gravel workings. Turn L, upstream, crossing a feeder and continuing on a straight path through trees along the built-up bank of the Giffre, swift-flowing and in the whole Haute-Savoie only second in size to the Arve. Ignore a footbridge and emerge into a field and out onto D907.

If you have managed to keep clegs at bay until now, beware of the voracious species which inhabit this particular strip of shaded water-side! Cross the Giffre at

● 1h – **PONT PERRET** 727m (2385ft) – *water, bus stop for Sixt and Samoëns.*

Proceed up the lane, past Les Faix chalets, once a sawmill, and along a track in forest, gently descending to cross a meadow. Ahead, the Giffre pours unexpectedly through a narrow, rocky ravine 100ft deep, and the little metal footbridge provides an excellent viewpoint.

GR5 now climbs through majestic beech woods, reminiscent of England, before leading the walker up the Gorges des Tines, the original bed of the infant Giffre. It is a sensational and geologically fascinating section, well waymarked throughout, threading up between scalloped limestone cliffs, scoured once by glacial meltwater. Three rock steps are climbed by fixed metal ladders.

The trail finally descends through woods and meadows to a road by a group of barns. The Collet d'Anterne, our next climb, is visible ahead beneath the jagged summit of Pointe de Sales, 2496m (8189ft). Turn L over the Giffre, promptly R, then L up between chalets to a tiny chapel in the centre of

● 1h – **LE FAY** 765m (2510ft) – *water. (20 min NE – SIXT – supplies, bar, restaurants; Gîte de Sixt (20 places, guardian 15/4 to 15/12, bedding and kitchen equipment, showers, toilets); tourist information, telephone, buses for Samoëns: 13th-century abbey church.)*

Sixt is the gateway to the Fer à Cheval cirque at the head of the Giffre valley, a huge rampart of summits and passes from Mont Ruan 3047m (9996ft) and le Buet 3099m (10,167ft) to the Sageroux Pass 2404m (7887ft). From the roadhead at Plan du Lac, it is a two-hour walk to view the cirque and surrounding peaks – les Dents Blanches, Mont Ruan's glacier, the Pointe de Finive and Pic de Tenneverge; and there are numerous waterfalls.

From le Fay there are two alternative routes to Pont de Sales – back down R across meadows and along the Giffre's E bank, or up to Maison Neuve and R along the D290 to

● 20m – **SALVAGNY** 857m (2812ft) – *bars, cafe-restaurant, hotel, water, telephone, Auberge de Salvagny (50 places, meals, open May-Sept.)*

The two alternatives from le Fay converge where riverside path meets road at a barn one kilometre beyond an information board. Cross the Giffre (yet again!), go round a bend and turn L up a stony track, crossing a boulder-choked torrent bed to rejoin the road at the stunning sight of the

● 45m – **CASCADE DE ROUGET** – *car parking.*

After heavy rain and early in the season, an immense volume of white water roars over two rock steps 70m (over 200ft) high, causing curtains of spray to drift across the area.

Continue a short way up the road, watching for the first of several pretty little paths which short-cut the road dog-legs. Pass the Chalets de Fardelay (possible shelter/camping) and reach the roadhead at

● 40m – **CHALETS DU LIGNON** 1177m (3861ft) – *car parking.*

A large sign on the path advertises the Sales and Anterne refuges, after which you climb steadily in and out of forest up rugged mountainsides to a magnificent complex of waterfalls, the

● 45m – **CASCADES DE PLEUREUSE & LA SAUFFLA** 1450m (4757ft) – *close to the junction with GR96 which leads to the Refuge de Sales (36 places, guardian 1/7 to 15/9, bedding and kitchen equipment, meals and drinks).*

The GR96 variant ahead ascends through the Sales gorge to the refuge, a popular base for climbing on the vast Désert de Platé and several peaks in the vicinity. On a fine summer weekend, this path carries a steady stream of climbers, walkers and day-trippers.

GR5 turns L at the path junction, however, on a stony track, becoming more earthy on the steep, scrubby slopes leading to

● 1h – **COLLET D'ANTERNE** 1800m (5905ft) – *viewpoint, wild camping possibilities.*

From the col are wonderful views, down over the Giffre valley and back to Col de la Golèse. To the NE is the Frêtes du Grenier, with the Grenarion Refuge perched high on its flanks. But most special of all, if you are fortunate with the weather, is the sight of Mont Blanc, seen due south over the snow-streaked slopes of Col d'Anterne.

GR5 proceeds through alders and descends an area of boulders to cross the Anterne torrent. It threads through rocky outcrops then over marshy ground; in mist, follow the R bank of the Anterne torrent and at its first L fork follow the stream up – this runs parallel with, and not far from, the path, past sheepfolds, to the

● 30m – **REFUGE ALFRED WALLIS** 1808m (5932ft) – *70 places, guardian 25/6 to 15/9 dormitories with blankets, tables and gas cooking, drinks, meals. (Appears as Chalets d'Anterne on some maps.)*

From the refuge, take a path-branch R (due S) which climbs across scree slopes, steep in places, zig-zagging out and over grassier slopes and down R across a depression to the beautiful

● 50m – **LAC D'ANTERNE** 2060m (6758ft) – *wild camping.*

The lake has no visible outlet, its waters disappearing into a limestone fissure. It is a popular destination for fishermen and day-walkers

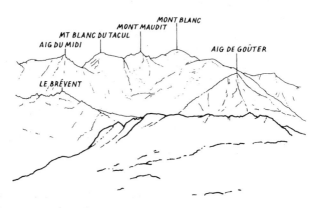

*VIEW SE FROM COL D'ANTERNE*

and there are superb possibilities for wild camping on its flat N and E shores. Sometimes you can hear rockfalls from the massive face of Tête a l'Ane to the W.

GR5 follows the E shore southwards, climbing round L of higher ground (shown on maps as spot height 2191m (7188ft)), where you cross several streams and snowfields of various size and condition, depending upon the time of year and the previous winter's snowfall. The gradient, however, is never steep and leads straightforwardly to the wooden cross L of a conspicuous vertical cliff at the

● 40m – **COL D'ANTERNE** 2264m (7428ft) – *panoramic viewpoint par excellence!*

In clear weather there is an unforgettable panorama to the south. Beyond and above the Aiguille Rouges and the Brévent ridge are the high snows of Mont Blanc, loftiest peak in western Europe at 4807m (15,771ft). To the W, the 1000ft cliffs of the Rochers des Fiz form a fortress-like corner with the Pointe d'Anterne, 2733m (8966ft). Like the Porte du Lac Vert before, this viewpoint is of a very special order, and it is well worth waiting for a clearance in bad weather, if you can, before reaching it.

From the col, a steep rocky path descends in zig-zags, across a gully, swings E at a junction and down to the

- **30m – CHALET-REFUGE DE MOËDE-ANTERNE** 1996m (6548ft) – *120 places, guardian 1/7 to third Sunday in Sept., dormitories with blankets, meals, drinks, (crowded in season); possibilities for wild camping on grassy levels.*

A clear track descends first SW, then back E above the small Laouchet lake. It passes below the Chalets de Moëde, following down the L bank of the Moede torrent amidst extravagant wild flowers (not all alpine varieties are small!). The path turns NE at the Tête de Jeubont, descending all the time, to reach the

- **1h – PONT D'ARLEVÉ** 1597m (5239ft).

This little bridge, which is removed each autumn and replaced at the start of summer, spans the Diosaz torrent, which plunges through deep gorges downstream on its way to join the Arve near Servoz.

GR5 now turns S and climbs along dry, bushy slopes before crossing a region of numerous streams, draining the Noir and Cornu lakes above. Pass the ruinous Chalets d'Arlevé (rough shelter) and in just over one kilometre reach an important, waymarked

- **1h 15m – PATH JUNCTION** 2018m (6621ft).

Ahead, the track traverses the Coquille mountain, eventually rising to the Brévent ridge south of the Lac du Brévent. GR5, however, turns L here, up increasingly steep and rocky slopes but on a superbly graded path, so that although the climb is a strenuous one, you are taken economically up through boulders and across snow patches to the often snow-covered

- **1h – COL DU BRÉVENT** 2368m (7769ft) – *splendid views back to Col d'Anterne; escape route SE to Plan Praz.*

At this col, GR5 joins the route taken by the Tour du Mont Blanc ascending from the Chamonix valley, and the two trails are coincident for the next couple of days or so, to the Col de la Croix-du-Bonhomme. This adds inevitably to the volume of walkers, both on the paths and competing for overnight accommodation.

Turn R at the col, taking a well-trod line behind the precipitous E

*Pointe d'Anterne (left) and the Col d'Anterne (centre)
from the Col du Brévent*

slopes. The path threads rocks, sometimes scrambly, crosses snow patches and climbs to the summit of

● 1h – **LE BRÉVENT** 2526m (8287ft) – *bar/snacks (expensive!), viewing platforms and Touring Club de France view indicator. Access to Chamonix by téléphérique to Plan Praz and telecabin to the valley; possible shelter in téléphérique top-station buildings.*

Le Brévent is the first actual summit and the highest point reached so far on GR5, following a succession of higher and higher cols. It was first climbed in 1760 by a 20-year-old student. From here there is a classic view SE to Mont Blanc, the Aiguille du Midi, 3842m (12,605ft), and the courses of the huge Bossons and Taconnaz glaciers. In the N are the Aiguilles Rouges, NW the Sales Desert and Col d'Anterne, while below in the SW lies the Lac de Brévent.

Built in 1928–30, the téléphérique from Plan Praz to the Brévent summit was a feat of great engineering audacity, spanning 1348m (4422ft) and 515m (1690ft) of vertical height between the pylons. It was renewed in 1988. You can feel justifiably smug at having come up the hard way, but it ought to be said that the mechanical route makes an exhilarating ride and is not unduly expensive. It provides an effective escape route, or a pleasant excursion to the fleshpots of cosmopolitan

**CHAMONIX** – *all supplies, bars, restaurants, cafes, hotels, campsites, swimming pool, PTT, banks, doctor/pharmacies, buses (including the 'Chamonix-bus' valley service), SNCF, tourist information, mountain rescue, guides, museums, etc. The town plays host to well over one million visitors annually!*

From Le Brévent, descend the well-maintained stony path, following the ridge's undulations, with the lovely Lac du Brévent below R. There are airy, vertical views to the Chamonix valley 1150m (over 3500ft) below, yet the path is always safe with care. At a signed junction, turn L to the

● 50m – **REFUGE BEL-ACHAT** 2151m (7057ft) – *30 places, guardian 25/6 to 20/9, bedding equipment, meals and drinks; path L down to Chamonix via Plan Lachat (2h 30m).*

GR5 passes the scant remains of the original chalets before dropping steeply L, by numerous zig-zags and little rocky steps across the precipitous flanks of the Aiguillette du Brévent. This entertaining and dusty little path provides sensational views to the busy valley floor and across to the soaring heights of the Mont Blanc massif.

The entrance to the Mont Blanc road tunnel can be seen opposite, linking Chamonix with Aosta in Italy and passing beneath the Aiguille du Midi, Vallée Blanche and Pointe Helbronner for a total of 11.6 kilometres.

Soon the buildings of the Merlet nature reserve are in sight below and the path enters forest. At the reserve's perimeter fence, keep L down to a track near the entrance to

● 50m – **MERLET** 1562m (5125ft) – *drinks, meals, chance to see chamois, bouquetins, marmots etc. living in a semi-wild state.*

Follow the partly-surfaced track for about a kilometre but watch for the easily-missed path L at a waymarked tree. Continue down through forest, R at a bouldery junction, then L at an obvious fork to reach the Statue du Christ-Roi (Christ the King). This stands 17 metres high and contains a chapel in its base. It was erected in the 1930s following collections from locals and holidaymakers and is dedicated to peace.

Continue ahead to meet the road at chalets, turning down L. After a few bends, look for a waymarked path cutting the final dog-legs to the valley bottom. Cross the narrow-gauge railway at Les Houches station, pass a hydro-electric plant and risk life and limb getting to the far side of the busy N506! The road opposite leads quickly up to

● 1h 15m – **LES HOUCHES** 1008m (3307ft) – *all supplies, bars, cafes, restaurants, hotels, campsite, water, PTT, bureau de change, tourist information, doctor/pharmacy, buses for Chamonix, Grenoble, Annecy, Geneva and St. Gervais-les-Bains; and for Courmayeur via the Mont Blanc tunnel; SNCF; téléphérique to Bellevue; several gîtes/chalet-refuges.*

# ALTERNATIVE START TO THE GR5

**THONON-LES-BAINS** 431m (1414ft) – *all supplies, bars, cafes, restaurants, hotels, water, campsite, PTT, tourist information, bank, doctor/pharmacy, buses for Geneva, Annecy, St. Gingolph, Compagnie Générale de Navigation for Lac Léman, SNCF, mountain rescue.*

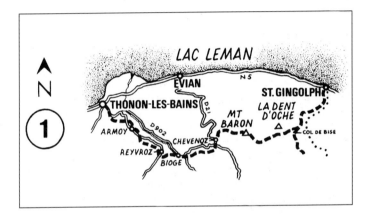

In the Stone and Bronze Ages, the settlement of Thonon was on the site of today's harbour – it was the Romans who discovered the benefits of its spring waters and established the famous spa.

The first waymarks begin (leaving the railway station) on the R in the Rue de Jean-Blanchard. Cross the footbridge and the Crête square to leave Thonon by the Trossy road, approaching the Forêt de Thonon. Take care not to confuse the GR waymarks with the forestry ones (red border on white).

Leaving the broad Vionnaz track to the R, continue SE over level ground and take a track L (E) to the forest edge. It rises into oak and chestnut trees R, up to the l'Ermitage road. Cross and in 5 mins reach la Pépinière, a paddock beneath large cedars once used as a tree nursery. The trail runs alongside on a lane and in about 100 metres turns L. After passing a forestry shelter, it climbs R into oak and beech woods and, after two bends in the path, arrives at a glacial terrace with good views back over Thonon and Lac Léman. The route crosses the Lonnaz road, drops into a shady combe rising E to the Compte-Rouge crossroads. Carry straight on up to the old road from Thonon to Armoy. Turn L then R to reach the new road (D26), following it L for a short distance before turning off R (NE) and R (S), at first in forest then on the edge of cultivated land to arrive at

● 1h 30m – **ARMOY** 645m (2116ft) – *limited provisions (inc. bread), hotel/restaurant, buses for Thonon and Bellevaux, telephone.*

GR5 passes below the church with parts dating from 1085; the transept was demolished during the French Revolution, rebuilt, then burned down in 1913 by a terrible fire that destroyed most of the village. Carry straight on along a forestry track and in 100 metres rise to the edge of the ancient woods (once used to supply firewood for the rectory). On a broad earthy track, the trail follows the wood's upper perimeter, veering S on the level to the head of a small combe. Join another forestry track (red border on white waymarks) up to a newer track, turning R in pine trees to climb the ridge onto the D26 road.

Turn right then take a track off to the left. Continue E on a surfaced road becoming an earth track and gradually climbing between rows of ash and hazelnut trees. You then contour the forested NE slopes of Mont d'Hermone, parallel to the D26 below. After passing near a chapel, fork R, first in forest then over open ground, swinging S, past the path junction with the 'Tour de Léman' and reaching

● 1h 30m – **REYVROZ** 776m (2546ft) – *limited provisions, restaurants, PTT, buses for Thonon and Bellevaux.*

Pass in front of the church, round the cemetery and down to the bottom of the village. Over the crossroads (D26) in the direction of Vers-le-Pré, take the path (with care) above the Brevon river. Follow this ancient road east, now a beautiful track (if wet in places) and descend steeply to

● 45m – **BIOGE** 528m (1732ft) – *buses for Thonon, Morzine and Châtel.*

The hamlet sits at the confluence of the Dranse de Morzine, the Dranse d'Abondance and the Brevon rivers before they rush, now as the Dranse itself, into the deep gorges towards Lac Léman. Not surprisingly, Bioge is a canoe/kayak centre.

Turn right onto the D902 and in 300m turn left over the 17th-century Dranses bridge. Cross the D22 and take the path into woods opposite. At the next junction bear right to exit the woods and reach the D21 at

● 40m – **LA PLANTAZ** 774m (2539ft).

Cross the D121 and take the stony track opposite for 100m, entering an earthy path off the bend to approach the cross at Les Granges. Bear right and here, at a new cross-junction, keep straight on along level ground to

● 30m – **LES CLOUZ** 900m (2953ft) – *hotel, camping, provisions, café, restaurant, buses.*

The GR5 now passes Théry hamlet, meets the D121 then drops on a shady track to

● 35m – **MÉROU** 820m (2690ft).

Cross the D121 and take the road descending left (NE). Further ahead the route crosses the Ugine valley by footbridge then climbs out up a steep, rough path through woods to the D32. Cross over and continue climbing, turning right on a lane and entering the hamlet of

● 45m – **LE CRÊT** 882m (2894ft).

Follow the road round NE (fork right for Chevenoz if provisions are required) as it climbs towards Prebuza. Beyond a reservoir turn off left onto a forest path, being careful to watch for waymarks on this section. At the exit from the forest, a permissive path takes you over pasture to

● 45m – **CHALETS DES TRABLES** 1115m (3658ft) – *water (no camping). Good views over the Jura, Lac Léman and, in the foreground N, the vast Gavot plateau overlooking Evian.*

GR5E continues to climb E in meadows, past a chalet R, to reach the Grands Bois forest, proceeding up to the mountain-pasture chalets of

● 30m – **LE PETIT and LE GRAND CHESNAY** 1320m (4331ft) – *water, possible shelter. (A path S, then W, leads in 15mins to the summit of les Trables 1420m (4659ft)).*

On a wide track which becomes a path and disappears in places, the route crosses a shallow depression E and reaches a small pine wood. Climb into more meadows, past a chalet at spot-height 1414m *(water, possible shelter)* and round the edge of a grassy hill towards a cross. Mont Baron dominates the view ahead, but beyond lies the rocky mass of the Dent d'Oche. Still over pasture, the trail passes a small hollow, climbs ESE on an indistinct trod, avoiding rocks, crossing through a thin wood and emerging at a grassy col. Do not descend R, but take a path E more gradually down to the base of the cliffs under

● 40m – **MONT BARON** 1563m (5128ft) – *It is possible to climb to the summit up the grassy E ridge for beautiful and extensive views.*

The trail descends towards the locally named Col of the Bulls, continuing SE between meadows and woods on an intermittent trod along the Grandes Heures ridge. Aim for a grassy plateau, crossing it ESE to find a good path at the entrance to forest. Ignoring branch tracks, proceed along the ridge on a path churned up by sheep and, shortly after the top of a ski-tow, you will come to a path crossroads called

● 30m – **COL DES QUEFFAIX** 1521m (4990ft) – *not named on some maps.*

Following waymarks, do not pass beneath the ski lift cables but instead take a path to the right (SE), climbing to the R of the top station. Beyond is a stiff pull up to gain the

● 45m – **TÊTE DES FIEUX** 1772m (5814ft) – *superb views over the Vacheresse valley.*

The onward route heads E along the ridge crest and crosses a piste. Do not take the path leading up to Pointe de Pelluaz, but fork L (NE), contouring under a ski lift and dropping past the ruinous

● 1h – **CHALET VERT** 1755m (5758ft) – *not named on some maps; spring just above the chalet.*

Situated at the foot of the moraine cirque of Pelluaz's N face. The GR5 descends into the combe then climbs ENE (red waymarks) steeply up to the ridge, which it follows NE on a delightful path at the border between the Abondance and Evian districts (care needed in wet weather). Descend to a lower section, locally called

● 20m – **COL DE LA CAS D'OCHE** 1820m (5971ft) – *not named on some maps; 'cas' is local dialect for 'goat-herd shelter'.*

The trail drops L (still NE) into alder woods with wild raspberries, passes the foot of the rocky cliffs dominating the extensive mountain pastures ahead and arrives at the two

● 15m – **LACS D'OCHE** 1749m (5738ft) – *path junction with the 'Tour de Léman'. (To the E of the lakes a path leaves NNW, swings W then climbs steeply N, leading in 1h 30m to the Refuge de la Dent d'Oche, 80 places, guardian July, August and weekends in June and September, bedding and kitchen equipment, meals, toilet. The refuge is 15 mins from the summit of Dent d'Oche 2222m (7290ft).)*

The lakes are situated beneath a vast and impressive mountain cirque, comprising L to R the Dent d'Oche, the Planchamp d'Oche col 1999m (6558ft) and the Château d'Oche 2199m (7214ft), all of whose N faces are precipitous and inaccessible.

Pass round the N of the lower (northern) lake, partially choked with reeds, and climb E in the combe, over grassy and rocky slopes. In the upper combe the trail steepens beneath the Château d'Oche's S cliffs. To the R (S) there is an interesting gap through the mountain walls of the Darbon summits. Continue climbing to reach the

● 50m – **COL DES PORTES D'OCHE** 1930m (6332ft) – *a deep notch between the summits of Darbon to the SW and the Château d'Oche N.*

GR5E drops gently over rocky terrain under the SE cliffs of Château d'Oche overlooking the Darbon lake. In clear conditions there is a wide ranging view in the SE to the Swiss Dents du Midi and even to the Mont Blanc massif itself. The trail soon rises a little to reach the huge grassy hollow of the

● 30m – **COL DE PLANCHAMP** 1943m (6374ft).

GR5E now descends across pastures, over several small streams and arrives at the path junction with the main routing.

## STAGE TWO

# *THE CHAMONIX VALLEY TO THE ISÈRE*

### 3–5 days

The busy Chamonix valley is glimpsed behind you for the last time from the approaches to the Col de Voza, but the high peaks and glaciers of the Mont Blanc massif continue to dominate.

GR5 follows the Montjoie valley's patchwork of fields and hamlets up to lively les Contamines and past the Notre-Dame-de-la-Gorge sanctuary on the old Roman road, to cross the high Bonhomme and Croix-de-Bonhomme cols. Haute-Savoie is left for the Beaufortain region of Savoie.

Still relatively undeveloped, Beaufortain is a region of isolated farms, dairy herds and some of the most beautiful forests in Savoie, some with deer. Mountains are of moderate height but wild and rocky in character and on their slopes can be found Purple Gentian and Edelweiss, chamois, marmots and streams rich with rainbow trout. Since the 1950s, the region has been nudged towards the twenty-first century by the exploitation of so-called 'white-coal' – the all-important hydro-electric power.

Beaufortain is a very ancient cheese-producing area but, unlike others, has always made its dairy produce directly up in the pastures rather than in village or farmstead. The work is carried out in modest chalets called *muandes* and mobile milking stalls with canvas awnings can sometimes be seen dotted about. Cheese made in these conditions has a distinctive nutty flavour from the high-altitude flora.

Descending from the remote and rocky Col de Bresson, GR5 enters the Tarentaise region, one which has seen perhaps the most brutal trans-formations this century in all Savoie. A few decades have changed the civilisation of the mule to that of the helicopter and in some places the two still exist, side by side. In the past, Tarentaise was a region of intense

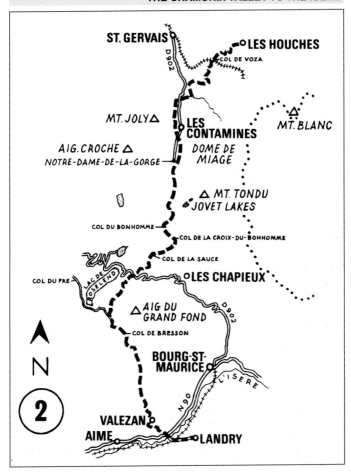

farming activity, despite the difficult climate. Rye was grown in many small fields and harvested just before the first snows, to continue ripening on the terraces. Large herds of hardy cattle climbed to high grazing, sometimes sinking to their shoulders in snowdrifts, and from the tender young grass gave – and continue to give – cheeses of great flavour.

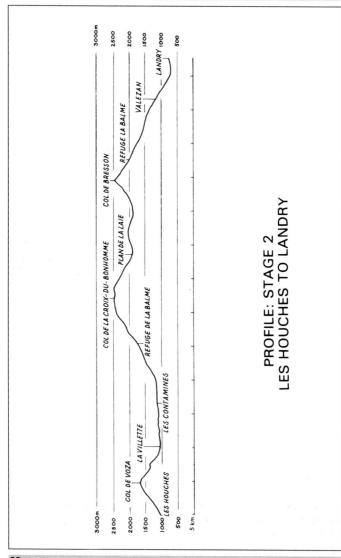

PROFILE: STAGE 2
LES HOUCHES TO LANDRY

The communes of la Côte d'Aime, Granier and Valezan (we pass through the latter) call themselves 'Le Versant du Soleil' (Hillside of the Sun). Their sheltered, south-facing aspect deprives them of long-lying snow for skiing and there has been a decline in agriculture and population. So the communes, like many others, are devising projects to attract the tourist – routes and facilities for walkers, and improved accommodation. A little agriculture, a little industry and a little tourism all help the valley to survive.

In fact, the Isère valley is a landmark of some significance for the south-bound walker. There are subtle changes in flora, fauna and architecture which herald the transition, soon, from Northern to Southern Alps. South-facing hillsides are drier, more brittle and loud with the chirping of crickets.

Proceed through Les Houches, over the Arve and up a track L just beyond the téléphérique station to Bellevue.

Cross a ski piste (Verte des Houches) and, arriving at a junction ahead, take the lane on the R. 100m beyond, after a little bridge over the Nant-Jorrand, the trail reaches another junction (several *gîtes* in the locality). Climb to the L and after the Maison Neuve ski lift join a good rising track which passes the chalets of la Tuile, la Cagotte and le Terrain, to reach

● 2h – **COL DE VOZA** 1653m (5423ft) – *bar, hotel and station for 'Tramway du Mont Blanc' which rises 2500m from the valley floor at Saint-Gervais-le-Fayet to the Bionnassay glacier, passing through tunnels, over viaducts and along rock ledges.*

*(NW – Hotel du Prairion, 19 places, meals, open during summer season)*

## Variant via Col de Tricot

Follow the tramway on a broad track SE from Col de Voza to Bellevue *(hotel-gîte)*, continuing round to the Chalets de l'Are above the Bionnassay valley. Here ignore the path heading S for the Nid d'Aigle and bear R (SW) down zig-zags to the terminal moraine of the Bionnassay glacier. Cross the meltwater torrent on a footbridge and ascend the moraine slope opposite. Continue SW up steep mountainside past the ruined chalets de Tricot to attain the

● 2h 15m – **COL DE TRICOT** 2120m (6956ft).

GR5 now descends relentlessly in zig-zags to

● 1h 15m – **CHALETS DE MIAGE** 1559m (5115ft) *(Refuge de Miage, 30 places, meals, camping, open June-Sept.)*

After crossing the Miage torrent on two bridges, the path trends W to reach

● 40m – **CHALETS DU TRUC** 1720m (5643ft) *(Auberge du Truc, 28 places, meals, open June-Sept.)*

The trail now takes to an ancient mule track (on which, alas, 4-wheel-drive vehicles are allowed), dropping through meadow and forest. Lower down it crosses a stream valley to the Granges de la Frasse and reaches

● 1h 15m – **LA FRASSE** 1263m (4144ft).

Short-cutting the downhill road bends between farmhouses and chalets, GR5 quickly arrives at

● 10m – **LES CONTAMINES-MONTJOIE** 1164m (3819ft).

## Continuation of Main Route
From Col de Voza, cross the tramway and descend a jeep track S, past car parking and joining a road down to

● 35m – **BIONNASSAY** 1350m (4429ft) – *(Refuge Auberge de Bionnassay, 15 places, meals, open all year)*, water, car parking, road access from D902.

The hamlet is full of lovely old chalets and to the E rises the Dôme de Goûter above the Bionnassay glacier. GR5 turns L before the refuge, past a tiny chapel (worth a peep inside) and down to the Bionnassay torrent, crossed by bridge. Climb into lovely larch woods, emerging onto a level track, along which turn R to the hamlet of Le Champel *(gîte, open all year)*. Turn L down a lane, L again off the first hairpin and proceed down to

● 1h 15m – **LA VILLETTE** 1055m (3461ft) – *water.*

The Montjoie valley ahead leads the eye beyond meadow and

settlement to a mountain barrier, soon crossed by GR5 at the Col du Bonhomme.

Cross the Miage torrent at the top of La Gruvaz hamlet. (More direct progress is possible by continuing on lanes to Tresse, but this does entail walking along the busy D902 for about 1 kilometre.)

The two alternatives rejoin by a shop where the trail takes a lane down to cross the Nant, bearing R up and round through chalets onto a pretty path giving superb views of the mountains opposite. Pass the track to Mont Joly and join a metalled lane. At a junction over a stream, turn L over the Nant, take a path R up to the road, turn R and in about one kilometre you arrive at

● 1h 40m – **LES CONTAMINES-MONTJOIE** 1164m (3819ft) – *all supplies, bars, cafes, restaurants, several gîtes, hotels, campsite, water, PTT, bank, tourist information, doctor/pharmacy, buses for St. Gervais and le Fayet. (Last supplies until the Isère Valley.)*

Continue S, straight through the town to a bridge over the Nant where the route from Nivorin converges and a good track makes a beeline along the L bank of grassy river flats to the popular

● 50m – **NOTRE-DAME-DE-LA-GORGE** 1210m (3970ft) – *cafe.*

This rather surprising baroque monument is a place of frequent pilgrimage, especially on August 15th (Assumption Day). Inside the

*Notre-Dame-de-la-Gorge*

*Hikers heading for the Col du Bonhomme*

typically Savoyard sanctuary is an altar-piece with twisted columns in the Italian Renaissance style and a register containing the signatures of Lord Byron and Victor Hugo.

The long climb to the Col du Bonhomme starts here, once a Roman road and now busy with walkers and 4-wheel-drive vehicles supplying high chalets. One such is the

● 45m – **CHALET DE NANT BORRANT** 1460m (4790ft) – *35 places, meals, open mid-June to end-Sept., possibility of camping, water.*

The trail now crosses a vast area of open pasture, climbing gradually to reach

● 45m – **CHALET-GÎTE LA BALME** 1706m (5597ft) – *50 places, meals, open mid-June to mid-Sept., camping.*

Above the refuge buildings, leave the Roman road/jeep track for a path S, signed Col du Bonhomme, which climbs to pass a junction L for the Jovet lakes and emerges onto flatter terrain. Continue on the torrent's R bank, forking R at a concrete sluice. Ignore a thin, waymarked trod R which makes a pointless little climb, keeping instead to the broad track to cross a stream.

GR5 climbs more steeply now, out onto another small plateau at a huge cairn at Plan des Dames. Tradition has it that an 'English lady' and her companion were killed here by a violent storm. In memory of the tragedy and to ward off evil, add a stone of your own before passing.

With the col in view ahead, cross a possible snowfield and thread up shaley slopes on either the lower or upper paths which meet to make the final ascent up gravelly gullies and perhaps over more snow to the

● 2h 15m – **COL DU BONHOMME** 2329m (8146ft) – *views, hut shelter.*

The hut offers shade or shelter. The col itself is a graceful saddle giving new and exciting vistas of mountains ahead in good weather. In bad conditions it can be a bleak place indeed. To the E (L) is the two-headed rock called the Bonhomme et la Bonne Femme. To the N is the long Montjoie valley just ascended, NE the Tré-la-Tête massif, S and SW the Chapieux valley and Beaufortain mountains, and SE the Tarentaise and Mont Pourri.

Turn L (S) up a rocky path contouring rugged slopes which nevertheless hold rare and delicate alpine flowers in nooks and crannies. After crossing possible snow patches and small streams, bearing SE, the path leads out to the tall cairn on the

● 50m – **COL DE LA CROIX-DU-BONHOMME** 2483m (8146ft) – *Refuge du Col de la Croix-du-Bonhomme (100 places, guardian 15/6 to 15/9, all facilities, located 10 mins SE of col); camping possible, water, viewing table. (1h 45m SE – Refuge des Chapieux, 10 places, guardian during summer, bedding and some kitchen equipment; also Refuge de la Nova, 41 places, guardian 20/6 to 30/9, bedding, meals. Both refuges are reached by the Tour of Mont Blanc path to les Chapieux, 1554m (5098ft), via the Chalets de Plan Varado and de la Raja).*

At this high and impressive mountain location, GR5 bids farewell to the TMB trail and to the Department of Haute-Savoie and takes a line W of S, clearly leading (in good visibility!) to the foot of the Crête des Gittes. The path, after a narrow start, is exquisitely and securely cut into the rocky ridge (by a regiment of mountain infantrymen earlier this century) and winds airily from side to side of the crest, providing an absolutely sensational hour of high-level walking. (If snow covers the path on the northern side, it is better to follow the arête itself which is often free of snow.) The Mont Blanc massif fills the NE impressively, Mont Pourri the E and there are glimpses of the Roselend lake to the SW.

Beautiful alpine flowers abound, despite the unpromising shaley rock and in good weather this is a section not to be missed. (In very windy or stormy weather, it might be advisable to drop down SE to Les Chapieux and rejoin GR5 at Plan de la Lai by a lengthy but safer walk up the D902.)

The path climbs under the ridge's summit, then on down to the

● 1h 15m – **COL DE LA SAUCE** 2306m (7565ft).

One of several easy paths can be followed down L over grassy pasture. Keep L of Bel Air chalet *(water and dairy produce)* (sign R to Rocher du Vent) and descend more steeply, the D217 road now visible below. At the levels approaching the road (wild camping), continue ahead through chalets over a stream, along a track and over a torrent to reach the

● 1h – **REFUGE DU PLAN-DE-LA-LAIE** 1815m (5955ft) – *20 places, 15/6 to 15/9, bedding and kitchen equipment, meals, drinks; road access, car parking.*

Before the construction of the Roselend dam, GR5 descended to the village of Roselend, branching L to follow the now flooded Treicol valley. Consequently, FFRP had to find and establish a new routing to Treicol hamlet and this now traverses the lower slopes of the Aiguille du Grand Fond, providing the walker with magnificent views of the vast, man-made lake.

Cross the road at the refuge, turning L up a track and forking R past an old then a newer chalet. *(In 10min pass the Refuge de Plan Mya, 15 places, meals, open mid-June to mid-Sept.)* When the motorable track ends, turn L (S) uphill across pasture, ignoring a trod ahead over a knoll. This section is scantily waymarked.

Pass a cairn and cross a stream to climb a steeper path up the side of a previously unsuspected little valley. There are more delightful flowers, and dwarf rhododendrons too, acting as a foreground to retrospective views right back to a receding Mont Blanc, visible over the Col de la Sauce. The trail emerges onto flatter pasture, whereupon take a R fork and arrive at the

● 1h – **CHALET DE PETITE-BERGE** 2071m (6794ft) – *the second chalet of the same name.*

Turn half-L and contour the E side of a large marshy depression on a sometimes boggy path, cross a stream in a small ravine and reach a saddle, L of a breast-shaped hill, to find the

● 30m – **CHALET DE GRANDE-BERGE** 2055m (6742ft).

Continue ahead through dock, down towards a small waymarked ruin but short-cut easily L over a stream. GR5 then undulates pleasantly along the mountainside above the turquoise waters of the Roselend lake *(possibilities for wild camping).*

Arriving at an ancient chalet (Durrand), there are sudden and exciting views ahead up the Treicol valley to the mountain barrier which we are soon to cross.

Continue down, more steeply at a waymarked rock, to pick up a good path leading L from the Treicol chalets *(water, dairy produce, possible shelter)*. This stretch is easily confused by many cattle trods – if necessary, just keep descending steepish grassy slopes, thick with flowers, keeping L and above the conspicuous track on the valley floor. The correct waymarked path will inevitably be picked up, then followed SE over streams to eventually meet the ascending valley track. This now zig-zags easily up round the SE flank of the valley head to cross the Treicol torrent at a waterfall. Look for a path off left 1km before the waterfall to reach the

● 1h 30m – **RUINES DE PRESSET** 2011m (6598ft) – *possible shelter.*

Keeping R of the chalet, veer L at a waymarked boulder. (Path off R leading SW to the Col du Coin.)

GR5 now climbs steadily, the pastoral Beaufortain landscape

*The Refuge du Presset (distant left) beneath the
Aiguille de la Nova, from Col du Bresson*

opening out below, sheep replacing cattle. It is important to follow the
waymarking carefully, especially if snow is still lying, as the approaches
to the Col de Bresson are obscured by the chaotic and rugged terrain.

Turn R at a large boulder then keep well L on a good path threading
up rocky slopes. If on course, a yellow sign on a rock points up to the
'Tête a lion'. There above, perched on top of a cliff, is a highly real-
istic, but quite natural, profile of a lion's head.

The trail continues to zig-zag up the L side of a valley choked with
rocks and boulders towards the jagged and apparently impregnable
ridge ahead, keeping you guessing (as it has throughout the ascent)
about the line it will take. The conspicuous col to the R is ignored and
instead an intriguing little route up to the L finally unravels the mystery
as Col de Bresson hoves into sight.

● 1h 30m – **COL DE BRESSON** 2469m (8100ft) – (*20 mins NE, situated on a mound protected from avalanches and overlooking the
Presset lake, Refuge du Presset (22 places summer and winter,*

*unguarded, bedding and kitchen equipment, wood-burning stove.))*

To the S of the col, the Pierra Menta monolith stands sentinel over the ridge. Legend has it that Gargantua stumbled over these crumbling peaks whilst roaming the Alps and, in his rage, kicked the offending rock to its present position! To the SE stands Mont Pourri and all around are snow-filled gullies and vast slopes of rock and scree.

GR5 descends half-R over loose ground, crossing meltwater streams and becoming a good path down by the gurgling, splashing Ormente torrent. Pass a small shelter and descend round E to the

● 1h – **CHALET DE LA BALME** 2009m (6591ft) – *25 places summer and winter, guardian 1/7 to 15/9, meals, bedding in communal dormitory, cooking pans, gas, meals and drinks, water.*

Turn L past the building on a rough, motorable track S. At the first bridge, do not cross the Ormente but continue straight ahead on a waymarked path along the river's L bank (not along the road, as shown on some maps). Good opportunities for wild camping.

Having reached some large modern barns opposite Forand hamlet, continue descending beside an irrigation channel serving Valezan.

At the remarkably beautiful and old Les Fours chalets, a breath-taking view opens up ahead. Across the Isère valley (still far below) are the peaks in the Vanoise National Park, ranged each side of the large cleft of the Ponturin valley up which GR5 climbs to the Col du Palet. Descend past a newer chalet and many older, traditional ones, on a good track which eventually joins a metalled road for 200m before dropping R on a track to another road at the top of picturesque

● 2h 30m – **VALEZAN** 1186m (3891ft) – *gîte (food, wine, open all year), water, road access.*

Descend the terraced slopes down waymarked alleyways, short-cutting road zig-zags and passing en route an 18th-century church, a war memorial, the Town Hall, a tiny chapel, several drinking troughs and numerous nervous dogs! At the bottom, descend a rougher track to a surfaced lane, turn L for 50 metres, then R and immediately L down a grassy track. After crossing a stream, bear L at a junction, R at a firmer track, then promptly L down by a stream. The little path contours the hillside before dropping to emerge at le Grey hamlet, with its fascinating chapel. When the road bends R, cut down L on a path into

*The ancient les Fours chalets on the descent into the Isère valley*

● 1h – **BELLENTRE** 776m (2546ft) – *provisions, café, water.*

Turn L along the N90 (probably encountering the first heavy vehicles seen since Chamonix) and turn R down a side road to the Isère river, cutting final bends on a path. At the new bridge (the old one was undermined by floods in 1983), GR5 reaches its lowest height above sea level (719m, 2359ft) since Lac Léman and will not plumb such depths again until St. Sauveur-sur-Tinée in the Alpes-Maritimes.

Cross the Isère, turning L on the D220; pass over the railway (it ends not far to the E at Bourg-St.-Maurice) and walk through Les Granges hamlet, past allotments and orchards. Shortly after the road junction R to Montchavin, turn R into

● 45m – **LANDRY** 777m (2549ft) – *provisions, bar, hotels, campsite, water, SNCF north of the village, buses for Peisey-Nancroix.*

Note: An alternative route from Bellentre to Nancroix crosses the Isère bridge and is then signed via Montchavin to Nancroix.

## STAGE THREE

# LANDRY TO MODANE

## Three variants through the Vanoise National Park

Still in the Tarentaise, we see its other face in some of the largest ski centres on earth – new resorts with spiders webs of ski-lift cables and pylons, attracting winter visitors by the thousand. The region is also a great producer of hydro-electric power, with the impressive Tignes dam at the northern end of the huge artificial Lac du Chevril. The future holds, perhaps, more hydro-electric schemes, and there has been prospecting for uranium…

It will come as some relief to the walker to discover that GR5 passes through an area of great natural beauty preserved from exploitation: the Vanoise National Park, set up in 1963 and first of a string of such ventures within France.

The trail climbs from the deep trench of the Isère valley, through picturesque Peisey-Nancroix below the famous Les Arcs skiing centre, and follows the Ponturin torrent out into high mountain country for a long but easy crossing of the Col du Palet. Thereafter the walker has three official variants from which to choose a route to Modane:

a) **GR55** – From above Tignes, a high mountain passage via the Col de la Leisse, the alpine resort of Pralognan-la-Vanoise and the lofty Col de Chavière (highest point reached by the GR55 trail). Most of the route is between 2000m and 2600m (6500ft–8500ft) and, apart from Pralognan, the only sources of shelter and sustenance are refuges, camping within the Park not being allowed. Snow covers the higher stretches until late in the season and sometimes all summer. The compensations for experienced mountain walkers, however, include the likelihood of seeing bouquetins, chamois and marmots at close quarters and the chance to travel through remote and beautiful mountain country. About four days to Modane.

b) **GR5** – Passing through Tignes and the famous ski resort of Val d'Isère, the trail climbs over the Col d'Isèran (highest point on GR5),

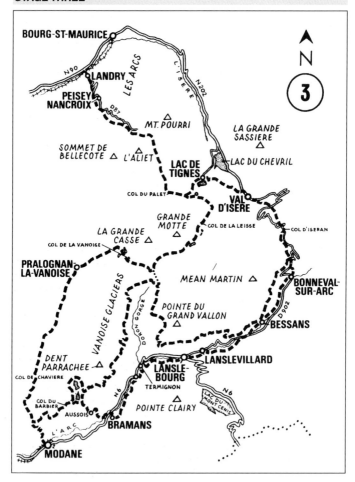

descending to a junction above the Arc valley. Thence, a mid-height route is followed, using a natural shelf above the valley at around 2000m (6500ft) on the edge of the Park. A big loop is made N round the Doron gorge, then back S along wild and rugged mountainsides beneath the Arpont glacier and la Dent Parrachée. The trail passes two artificial lakes before crossing the Col du Barbier and descending to Modane. Apart from a temporary descent to the Arc valley at Bessans, the walker must rely on refuges for shelter as camping is forbidden within the Park boundary. Although several paths link with valley towns and villages, these involve hefty descents and subsequent ascents to rejoin the trail. About 6 days to Modane.

c) **GR5E** – Following GR5 (above) to the junction above the Arc valley, this variant drops to Bonneval-sur-Arc to link the fascinating Haute-Maurienne villages of Bessans, Lanslevillard, Lanslebourg-Mont-Cenis, Termignon, Solières-Sardières, Bramans and Aussois. The Arc valley is farmed and forested in places and offers a refreshing change from high mountain scenery for those interested in vernacular architecture of a particularly rich variety. At Aussois, the route climbs to join GR5 at the artificial lakes and over the Col du Barbier to Modane. About 5 days to Modane.

Much of the Vanoise is composed of sedimentary rock which has been extensively eroded. Indeed, the area's present relief is largely the result of the processes of erosion, deposition and collapse. Glaciers have been responsible for shaping the land, and still are, although their influence hereabouts is greatly diminished since the times when they carved out whole valley sections. The Isère glacier alone once spread out west beyond Chambéry and Grenoble and only began retreating some 10,000 years ago.

Storm water, frost and melting snow are the main agents involved now, carrying material down from unvegetated, insecure slopes and depositing it in valleys as deltas or cones of alluvium. In this way, most of the original lakes occupying glacial valleys have been reduced in size or filled in and replaced by alluvial plains, though still easily recognisable (eg. the vestiges of lakes near the Berthoud and Grassaz chalets N of the Col du Palet).

An example of collapse occurs between Bessans and Lanslevillard where a vast landslip completely blocked the Arc valley, now crossed at the Col de la Madeleine. Behind this natural dam once lay a large lake, the bed of which forms the Bessans plain.

The lower Ponturin valley is steep-sided and comprised of schists and sandstone from the Carboniferous era. Here are mixed forests of broad-leaved trees which require rich, deep soil and plentiful moisture – mainly ash, hazel, oak and larch. In these woods and at the torrent's

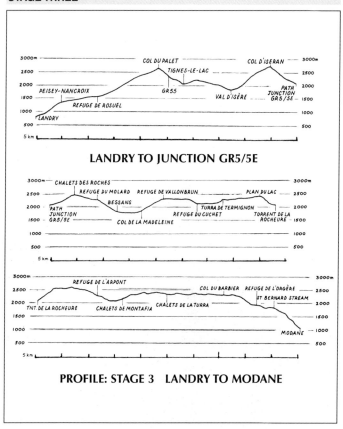

**PROFILE: STAGE 3 LANDRY TO MODANE**

edge, many plant species thrive, and in such a varied habitat common birds flourish too. At the forest boundaries, buzzards and sparrow-hawks hunt their prey.

Higher up, the valley broadens out into a distinctive 'U' shape section, betraying its glacial origins. Higher still, a terrace links the hanging valley of the Nant Benin with that of the Ponturin, and the Bellecote cirque still retains some residual ice.

# MAIN ROUTE – GR5

Landry is another ancient village, with logs stacked for the winter and communal troughs used for washing clothes. Cross the Ponturin torrent and walk up the D87, past a camp. 100 metres after the first hairpin, take a path R, cutting the road corner. Continue up the road for 400 metres to a track R at the next hairpin. Cross a stream and climb the path L, cutting off a long road dog-leg. Back at the road, turn R for 200 metres then R onto a lane, keeping L at a tall shed and climbing to le Moulin hamlet. The conspicuous pointed peak ahead is the Aiguille de l'Aliet 3109m (10,200ft). At le Moulin, turn L for

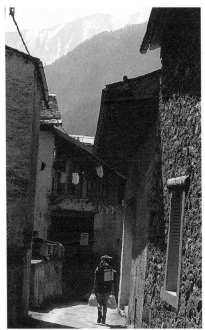

Stocking up at Peisey-Nancroix on the threshold of the Vanoise National Park

● 1h 30m – **PEISEY-NANCROIX** 1264m (4147ft) – *all supplies, bars, restaurants, hotels, water, campsite, PTT, tourist information, buses for Landry.*

GR5 takes a lane down R at le Moulin, over the Ponturin and up L alongside the torrent which tumbles picturesquely over boulders through pine trees. At a good track, turn L. *(For Nancroix village-hotel, some provisions – cross the Pont Romano bridge L).* Proceed along the track through forest and pass the Glières campsite. *(Over Pont Baudin is Gîte d'étape Les Glières, 30 places, open all year.)* Ahead L is the snowy summit of Mont Pourri 3779m (12,398ft) and an exciting array of snow-streaked peaks and ridges in the Vanoise National Park.

At the Glières campsite reception building, keep R along the edge of the trees past an old chalet, forking R before a large building. Turn L at a ruin, cross a torrent and walk R along the D87 past Les Lanches hamlet. E of the hamlet rejoin the old road over the Ponturin, through Bettières hamlet and back over the river to reach

● 1h 30m – **REFUGE DE ROSUEL** 11556m (5105ft) – *64 places, guardian 1/6 to 15/9, bedding and kitchen equipment, meals, car parking.*

*Refuge de Rosuel*

The refuge's architecture is a marriage of traditional materials with modern design, and the wave-shaped roof allows snow-slides to pass over it without causing damage.

Signs announce Col du Palet – 4 hours, which is about right. It is a long ascent, to the highest point reached so far on GR5, but is nowhere particularly steep and the trails in the Park are well frequented in season. The Ponturin valley head is still farmed simply – hay, goats, cattle; and the chalets have a great natural charm, constructed as they are from organic materials.

Take a track R up across stony slopes, then through alders and undergrowth opposite the Cascades de la Gurraz which feed the Tignes hydro-electric plant via an 8 kilometre underground gallery. The main cascade is an impressive and noisy 100 metre drop.

GR5 reaches a flatter area with larch trees where the bones of the mountain show through the thin turf. Follow the Ponturin stream up and fork L (signed) crossing it for the last time to gain

*TOWARDS THE COL DU PALET*

● 1h 30m – **CHALET DU BERTHOUD** 2091m (6860ft) – *used by Park wardens. (45min along the W bank of the Ponturin stands Refuge Entre-le-Lac, 45 places, open mid-June to mid-Sept.)*

Soon the trail approaches a large sign bearing the Vanoise National Park regulations. They have been formulated to protect the flora and fauna so it will come as no surprise that picking flowers, camping, and dogs (even on a lead) are not allowed.

Cross marshy levels, past a path L to the Mont Pourri refuge and another to the Col de Sachette further on. The Chalets de la Plagne hut is surrounded by ancient enclosures, now overgrown with dock.

Threading easily up through rock outcrops, the emerald green Lac de la Plagne slides into view below R, a well-used path leading along its far shore from the junction back near the Berthoud chalet. (This path continues SW to the Refuge de Plaisance as well as allowing access to an ascent of the S side of l'Aliet.)

Up here you will hear the whistling cry of marmots and with luck or patience will see them too. These charming, furry creatures, up to 60cms (2ft) in length, hibernate from mid-October to mid-April. They seem quite numerous and watch us humans approaching with a mixture of curiosity and caution before disappearing into their burrows.

The trail continues up and over to a vast shallow depression and the ruins of the

● 1h 15m – **CHALET DE LA GRASSAZ** 2335m (7661ft) – *water.*

*Marmot*

The approaches to the Col du Palet are now visible ahead, with the high, snowy dome of La Grande Motte (3653m/12,085ft) rising above and beyond. Pass a path L to Col de la Tourne and follow GR5 on up steeper slopes to the Lac de Grattaleu, crossing the outlet stream and walking along the lake's R (W) shore to climb over a knoll ahead. *(10 mins NE – Refuge du Col du Palet, 48 places winter and summer, guardian 15/6 to 15/9, bedding and kitchen equipment, meals and drinks, camping during July and August.)* Ascend the final slopes, looking back for the last time down the long, deep cleft of the Ponturin valley and following the path which bears L up to the large flat

● 1h 30m – **COL DU PALET** 2652m (8701ft) – *panoramic views.*

Descend ahead, now in Haute-Tarentaise, until the path passes beneath the

● 25m – **TÉLÉSKI DE GRATTALEU** 2400m (7874ft) – *path junction for GR55 variant. Route notes for GR55 appear after GR5 notes reach Modane.*

Pass a track R leading to a ski-lift station, go over a rise then on down past the Croix de Lognan until the resort of Lac de Tignes comes into sight below.

Author's comments: Unless you are a dedicated skier, to whom nothing matters but the provision of pistes and the associated technology to hoist you up the mountains, Lac de Tignes and Val Claret will almost certainly offend. From GR5's elevated viewpoint, the tower-block hotels and apartments, ski-tows and chair-lifts, bulldozed pistes and access roads look like inner city development of the worst kind transplanted into a wild and beautiful mountain setting. The desecration is on a vast scale and all the more jolting for the GR5 walker fresh from the unsullied landscape of the Vanoise National Park (a temporary exit from which has just been made). No doubt Lac de Tignes looks attractive enough under a mantle of snow and no-one would deny the popularity and value to the region of the ski holiday industry. It does seem regrettable, however, that planning appears to be so piecemeal and out of sympathy with the natural environment. Just what you do about ski-lift hardware and the barren scars of pistes during the summer months is hard to fathom…

The lovely green lake, used for sailing and windsurfing, is some compensation for the descending walker; GR5 deposits you next to it on the road along its N shore. Turn L and enter

● 1h – **LAC-DE-TIGNES** 2093m (6867ft) – *all supplies, bars, cafes, restaurants, Chalets Internationaux de Haut Monatgne (20 places, meals), hotels, campsite, water, PTT, sports centre, gambling! car parking.*

Turn R along a street behind the vast array of tennis courts and at

*The snowy Dôme de Bellecôte and the pointed
l'Alliet from Col du Palet*

the end turn L up under a chair-lift. This section is poorly waymarked and the path, such as it is, is likely to change. Once climbing, however, it is clearer, zig-zagging up the slopes E of Tignes to emerge at the

● **40m – PAS DE LA TOVIÈRE** 2252m (7388ft) – *views, excellent in clear weather, with the S (Italian) flank of the Mont Blanc massif visible in the N, while back above Tignes is the glaciated Dôme de la Sache. La Grande Sassière lies NE across the huge Lac du Chevril (the Tignes dam caused a minor war with conservationists when it was proposed, but was built nonetheless and now supplies the Malgovert Regional Group with hydro-electricity). To the S stands the sentinel Rocher de Bellevarde, another mountain raped by the ski developers. The eroded cliffs W are la Tovière.*

Cross a rocky plateau (good wild pitches but scarce water) then descend the waymarked path, past several ruined chalets and, at one with a wooden cross, drop more steeply through larches, bearing R at a junction. Cross a stream (good wild pitch) and continue down towards Val d'Isère, skiing mecca, now visible as a ribbon of buildings straddling the busy D902. GR5 joins a broad track down to an electricity station on the valley floor, turning R, then L over the channelled Isère and along the main thoroughfare of

● **1h 45m – VAL D'ISÈRE** 1809m (5935ft) – *all supplies, bars, cafes, restaurants, hotels, campsite, water PTT, tourist information, bank, buses for Bourg-Saint-Maurice (SNCF).*

The town, as you might expect, is rather brash and up-market, with strange juxtapositions between old and new. Pass through E, turning R beyond the Gendarmerie (police station and mountain rescue post), then L, parallel to the D902. The trail passes above the campsite, through Le Laisinant settlement and up a signed track which soon becomes a path. Cross two streams in the Combe de Laisinant and climb the path (designated as a natural trail), turning R at a junction before zig-zagging up, in and out of forest, with superb views across to the Pointe du Santel and back over the Isère valley. The path climbs determinedly amongst wild flowers of great beauty to the D902, whereupon turn L then R to rejoin the ascent, past marmot burrows and over the Isèran torrent. Follow up its L bank, alongside a bare ski piste. Pass two stone pyramids, thereafter climbing less steeply and proceeding straight ahead (SSE) on muddy tracks, obliterated in places, to a ski-tow. It is hard to

*Pont de la Neige (natural snow bridge) below Col d'Isèran*

believe this area is a designated nature reserve! Continue climbing gradually and across the road's final zig-zag to arrive at the

● 3h 30m – **COL D'ISÈRAN** 2764m (9068ft) – *highest point on GR5 and second highest road pass in the French Alps; bar/restaurant, souvenirs, chapel (1939) with large statue of Notre-Dame-de-Toute-Prudence, stone shelter.*

The D902 crosses the Col d'Isèran (closed during the winter). Road access, with its attendant traffic and car parks, detracts from the quality of the col but not, perhaps, from the sense of achievement you feel from getting there on foot! There are extensive views to the E and S of countless peaks. Ahead lie the mountains and villages of Haute-Maurienne, close to the Tarentaise but very different in geology, wildlife, history and inhabitants.

From the large stone pyramid at the col, a rather steep and narrow path slants down R, re-entering the Vanoise Park and meeting the road near the

● 45m – **PONT DE LA NEIGE** 2528m (8294ft).

The snowbridge varies in size from year to year but is interestingly located next to the man-made road bridge. Providing you can cross the feeder torrent W of the road bridge, follow the narrow path beneath the steep face of the Ouille de la Jave down the Lenta gorge (beware possible stonefall). Cross the swift-flowing Lenta (rough bridge not guaranteed!) and climb its L bank to a marshy level. (If the feeder torrent W of the road bridge is too full to cross, continue walking down the D902 and watch for a GR waymark after about 500 metres at a steep little path R leading down to the same marshy level.)

The rather thin path now threads cunningly down above the Lenta gorge and leads to the two buildings near the road called

● 30m – **PIED-MONTET** 2274m (7460ft).

Cross the bridge and turn down R, following the delightful Lenta torrent's L bank, past ancient barns, to an important

● 20m – **JUNCTION OF GR5/GR5E** – *track ahead (SSE) for GR5E variant. (Route notes for GR5E appear after GR5 notes reach Modane).*

The track, R, signed 'Mollard Refuge', forks L, crosses a torrent and climbs easily W up a hillside. At the top, another sign confirms GR5's direction SE, then SW diagonally up across steepish mountainside beneath Pointe de la Met. This next section, to the Chalet des Buffettes, is across private land and not officially waymarked. It also traverses difficult terrain in places, although the Arc valley is never far away and can be reached by two paths. (An alternative would be to descend to Bonneval-sur-Arc on GR5E (well worth a visit anyway) and climb back up to GR5 by the Roches chalets.)

Keep to the more distinct of two trods initially, crossing several streams before negotiating a ravine and scree and reaching

● 1h 15m – **CHALETS DES ROCHES** 2453m (8048ft) – *path access (steep zig-zags E) to Bonneval-sur-Arc, approx 1h.*

A natural platform in the contours forms the basis for the entire route above the Arc valley, the 'Sentier Balcon de la Maurienne'. After the Chalet des Buffettes, GR5 passes below a large and spectacular cirque, with a waterfall issuing from the Méan Martin glacier above. It then descends to a bridge over the Vallon torrent, turns SE then S, passing a ruined chalet to arrive at

*Vernacular architecture and the Lenta Torrent below Col D'Isèran near the junction with GR5E*

- 1h 30m **LA CABANE DES GARDES DU MOLARD** 2230m (7316ft).

The trail descends to a

- 30m – **PATH JUNCTION TO LE VILLARON AND GR5E** – *(20 mins E – Gîte d'étape La Batisse, 36 places, guardian all year except Oct. and Nov., bedding and kitchen equipment, meals, drinks).*

GR5 descends towards Bessans in the broadening Arc valley below, past low cliffs to a wide riverside track leading over the bridge L and into

- 30m – **BESSANS** 1705m (5594ft) – *provisions, bars, hotels, campsite (the actual site, 'Les Chardonettes', is near the river 2 kilometres W). PTT, tourist information, buses for Arc valley and Modane, access to GR5E variant.*

Perhaps it is worth reminding readers that camping wild is not allowed within the National Park. The section to Modane is well endowed with refuges, but walkers intending to bivouac discreetly need to consider the supplies situation, since no settlement of any size is passed through unless a considerable descent and subsequent ascent are made to the Arc valley.

GR5 continues along the Arc's R bank on a good track. Beyond la Chalp, walk W for a short distance along the D902 before turning R, over the Refonderaz torrent and reaching

- 1h 15m – **COL DE LA MADELEINE** 1752m (5748ft) – *chapel, road access.*

Turn R at a sign to 'la Fesse d'en Haut and le Chatalard' on a path which proceeds to zig-zag steeply up the rough, scrubby slopes to

- 1h – **CHALETS DU MOLLARD** 2130m (6988ft) – *water, possible shelter.*

At a path junction, turn L (W), now following the perimeter of the Vanoise National Park again, past the Chapelle St. Antoine near la Fesse d'en Haut hamlet, arriving at the

- 30m – **REFUGE DE VALLONBRUN** 2272m (7454ft) – *45 places summer and winter, guardian 15/6 to 15/9, bedding and kitchen equipment.*

Continuing W for 1½ kilometres, the trail reaches buildings at la

Fesse-du-Milieu (possible path access S to valley) then crosses the valley of the Burel torrent, draining from the Vallonet glacier 1000m higher to the N. Cross a small valley and climb to a path junction. (R leads up to the neolithic Pierre aux Pieds.) GR5 crosses feeders of the Ruisseau de la Donnaz then contours W over several more streams.

*(Path, 1h SE, to Lanslevillard – supplies, restaurants, hotels, campsite, tourist information, buses for the Arc valley and Modane, access to GR5E variant.)*

Cross the Nay in its rocky valley, then the Plâtre, to the ruins of Primaria. *(Path, 1h S, to Lanslebourg-Mont-Cenis – all supplies, bars, cafes, restaurants, hotels, campsite, PTT, tourist information, buses for the Arc valley and Modane.)* Up to the R is the

- 1h 50m – **REFUGE DE CUCHET** 2160m (7086ft) – *24 places summer and winter, unguarded, bedding and kitchen equipment.*

The trail continues W under the cliffs and screes of the Grand Roc Noir's outliers, undulating through rocky outcrops, past ruinous les Rochasses, with spectacular views S across the Arc forest. It then descends gradually into the patchy Fontaniou woods to the chalets of Pré Vaillant and a path intersection. 1h SE drops to Lanslebourg (see above), 1h SW to Termignon – *(supplies, bar, restaurant, hotels, Gîte de Termignon, 32 places summer and winter, guardian 20/12 to 15/10, bedding and kitchen equipment, shower; campsite, water, PTT, tourist information, buses for the Arc valley and Modane, access to GR5E).*

GR5 takes the path R, zig-zagging up in a generally northerly direction to reach the Crête (ridge) de la Turra which forms a conspicuous and almost straight arm reaching down to Termignon from the Pointe du Grande Vallon 8 kilometres and 1830m (6000ft) up to the NE. Built on the very shoulder of the ridge are the

- 2h 30m – **CHALETS DE LA TURRA DE TERMIGNON** 2290m (7513ft).

From here the trail makes a big loop N round the Doron gorge, traversing on the southward leg some of the wildest and most majestic mountain scenery on GR5. The route undulates and crosses a variety of terrain, but there are no great changes of altitude involved and views are exceptional.

Leaving the Vanoise Park for 5 kilometres, GR5 crosses the Turra ridge NW before veering NNE, past Bercheren chalet and climbing

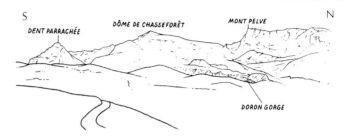

*VIEWS WEST AND NORTH FROM PLAN DU LAC*

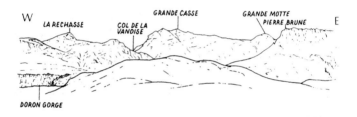

beneath extensive scree and over several streams. The trail gradually turns NW then W and reaches

● 1h 30m – **PARKING DE BELLECOMBE** 2307m (7569ft) – *road access from Termignon, summer shuttle services to and from the valley.*

Walk N briefly on the minor road but leave it soon for a parallel path R, past a lake and across the Plan du Lac to the

● 45m – **REFUGE DU PLAN DU LAC** 2364m (7756ft) – *60 places (30 in winter), guardian 10/6 to 15/9 and Easter and spring weekends, bedding and kitchen equipment, meals and drinks.*

There are outstanding views W over to the glaciers of the Vanoise and N to the Grande Casse, 3855m (12,647ft), highest peak in the Vanoise. By walking W from the refuge, a breathtaking view is obtained of the Doron gorge, often frequented by bouquetins while on the opposite flanks, amongst the moraines of the Mont Pelve glacier, may be chamois.

From the Plan du Lac, continue NNE, crossing the track (no private vehicles) at the Chapelle St. Barthélémy and zig-zagging down to rejoin it at the

● 30m – **TORRENT DE LA ROCHEURE** 2053m (6735ft) – *(15 mins N, path to the Refuge d'Entre-Deux-Eaux, 60 places, guardian 15/6 to 25/9, bedding and kitchen equipment, meals and drinks. From the refuge, it is possible by following the track N to join GR55 at the Pont de Croé-Vie).*

Do not cross the Rocheure torrent here (as shown on some maps), but follow the track along its L bank for about 800 metres and cross there. The track bends L to cross the torrent de la Leisse and reach the I'lle chalets. GR5 now turns R, then L, climbing in zig-zags the rather steep slopes of Mont de la Para. At the top of the steepish stretch is a path junction. R (N) leads off round the E slopes of the Plateau de la Réchasse, joining GR55 at a monument erected in memory of some alpine hunters, and on to the Refuge du Col de la Vanoise (see GR55 route notes for details).

GR5 makes a sharp turn L (SW), gradually climbing less steeply. Towards the last of the zig-zags, a few metres to the R, is a large carved stone, one of many in Haute-Maurienne thought to be the work of Neolithic man.

The trail passes near three small lakes, surrounded with rocks and boulders polished by the Pelve glacier. It then traverses a large area of moraines and crosses several streams. *(1h 30m return – an exceptionally beautiful high mountain location, the Ferran Lakes, 2720m (8924ft). Follow the moraine ridge W for about 2 kilometres before turning sharp R (NE). With luck you will see chamois and bouquetins at the foot of the Pelve glacier.)*

After crossing the undulating Pelve plateau, with the Refuge du Plan du Lac visible to the E across the gorge, the route cuts along the precipitous W wall of the Doron gorge. In normal summer conditions it is safe enough with care, but in heavy rain and especially should snow or ice cover the path, it becomes a potentially hazardous traverse in places. The trail veers W and descends to the

● 4h – **REFUGE D'ARPONT** 2309m (7571ft) – *90 places (28 in winter), guardian15/6 to 15/9, bedding and kitchen equipment, meals possible, bivouac possible.*

Marmots and bouquetins are often seen around the refuge.

GR5 passes near cattle enclosures at the Chalets de l'Arpont then crosses several streams to the Chapelle St. Laurent, L. There is another steep section after some ruins, before the trail descends gradually to the path junction at le Mont. *(Path L, 1h 30m to Termignon via the l'Esseillon chalets and D83 road.)* From here, bear W then SW, climbing up round the Combe d'Enfer over scree and rocky outcrops and crossing the Grand Pyx torrent, issuing from the Mahure glacier, by a small bridge. The trail then descends to

● 1h 15m – **CHALETS DE MONTAFIA** 2152m (7060ft) – *path L, 1h 30m to Termignon.*

The valley leading ahead to the Chalets de la Ferrière is easily crossed. After some zig-zags, climbing up under the cliffs of the Crête des Belles Places, GR5 ascends steadily then levels off SW, sometimes over grass, then over scree and rocks in a wild and impressive setting under the E flank of la Dent Parrachée. You drop a little to cross the Bonne Nuit ravine, shortly after which is another junction. *(Path L, 2h to Sollières, following down the Bonne Nuit at first, then through patchy forest.)* GR5 turns a ridge (falling E from the Pointe de Bellecôte) to reach the

● 1h 20m – **CHALETS DE LA LOZA** 2327m (7634ft) – *path L (S), 1h 30m to Sardières.*

From the small hill to the E of the path junction are wide views of la Dent Parrachée (W) and la Grande Motte.

In a SW direction, GR5 climbs and circles round above a rocky and eroded little valley before dropping in zig-zags to the ruins of the

● 1h 20m – **CHALETS DE LA TURRA** 2360m (7743ft) – *path L, 1h 30m to Sardierès, via the famous monolith.*

From here the path threads down rocky outcrops and is rather exposed in places, finally emerging onto more straightforward ground, though still steep, crossing stream valleys and leading SW to the

● 1h – **TÉLÉSIEGE DU DJOIN** 2230m (7316ft) – *(About 200 metres before the télésiege, a path R leads in 30m to the Refuge de Plan Sec, 80 places, open mid-June to mid-Sept); path access SW to Plan d'Aval lake and Aussois.*

GR5 turns R (N), above the upper lake (Plan d'Amont), passes la

Randolière chalet, crosses two streams and reaches a path junction at

- **30m – LA FOURNACHE** 2330m (7644ft) – *(Refuge de la Fournache, 21 places, guardian mid-June to mid-Sept.; 30 mins NW, Refuge de la Dent Parrachée, 29 places summer and winter, guardian in summer, bedding and kitchen equipment).*

Turning W, you come to another junction in 1½ kilometres. *(45 mins NW, Refuge des Fonds d'Aussois, 42 places, guardian in summer, bedding and kitchen equipment.)*

Drop down to cross the Pont de la Sétéria then climb SW, emerging onto a more level area with a path ahead snaking up the steep and rocky slopes of Col de la Masse. GR5, however, turns L (SE then S) above Plan d'Aval lake to pass through the

- **1h 30m – COL DU BARBIER** 2287m (7503ft) – *path junction with GR5E from Aussois, now coincident to Modane.*

The trail ascends gently to the Chalets du Barbier then levels off round a minor valley head (leading down to Bourget). There is a spring about 10 metres above the path. Descend along the edge of the Bourget forest, ignoring two paths off L but at the third, near the Chalets de l'Orgère, the trail turns N to traverse meadows, cross a stream, pass a chapel and immediately after arrive at a path junction. Climb up R to the D106 road and R to the

- **2h – REFUGE DE L'ORGÈRE** 1935m (6348ft) – *80 places (24 in winter), guardian 27/5 to 22/9, gas and washing facilities.*

GR5 now takes a nature trail SW, soon forking L on a forest track leading out to Pierre Brune. Continue W, cross the D106 and re-enter forest to reach the chapel in the hamlet of Polset and the

- **45m – RUISSEAU DE ST. BERNARD** 1770m (5807ft) – *path junction with GR55 from the north.*

Continue descending S, over meadows past la Perrière chalets, at which point GR5 deviates from following the torrent, swinging SE instead and dropping in steep zig-zags over quite rough and stony ground to arrive at Loutraz and, by a bridge over the Arc, into

- **1h 30m – MODANE** 1066m (3497ft) – *all supplies, bars, cafes, restaurants, hotels, campsite, PTT, tourist information, buses for the Arc valley and Chambéry, SNCF main line station.*

# GR55 VARIANT

From **TÉLÉSKI DE GRATTALEU**

*(If Lac-de-Tignes is to be visited, proceed along GR5 and exit it via Val Claret.)*

Aim for the Grande Balme téléski and follow it down to the bridge over the Retort stream near the Grande Motte telecabin station at the S end of

● 30m – **VAL CLARET** 2100m (6890ft) – *bars, shops, hotels, car parking.*

Take a line E, beneath the small Bollins téléski to pick up GR55 coming from Val Claret and Tignes, just before the Chalet de la Leisse. The trail climbs into the Vallon du Paquis by a L fork, past some small lakes and over above Chalet de Prariond veering S to the

● 1h 30m – **PATH JUNCTION TO COL DE FRESSE** 2531m (8304ft).

GR55 now climbs SW into an increasingly wild and barren mountain environment between the Grande Motte massif and the Pointe du Grand-Pré. Threading up through rocks, waymarking takes the form of cairns which need to be followed carefully, crossing snowfields lying late in the season, up to

● 1h – **COL DE LA LEISSE** 2487m (8159ft).

The col is dominated in the W by the Grande Motte glacier, while to the NE rise the great shining walls of la Grande Sassière.

From the col, GR55 descends through a shattered, eroded landscape (and again the cairns need to be watched for carefully) on a vaguely-defined track going S. Cross a feeder stream to the Lac des Nettes, below R, and its outlet, descending over grassier levels frequented by marmots. The trail becomes well waymarked and passes along the NW shore of the Plan des Nettes lake, past the small dam at its S end and drops down to the

● 1h 30m – **REFUGE DE LA LEISSE** 2487m (8159ft) – *48 places summer and winter, guardian in summer, bedding and kitchen equipment, meals.*

## PROFILES: GR55 and GR5E

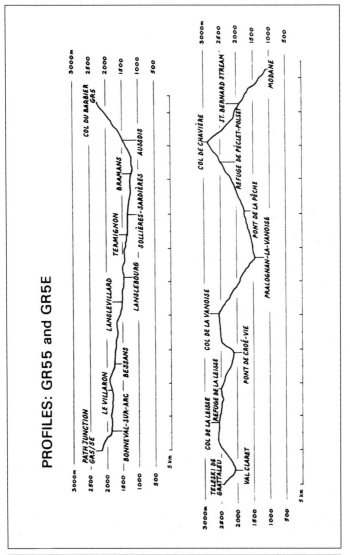

Boquetin or Mountain Ibex

Chamois

A little further down, WSW beyond the refuge, you cross the Leisse torrent and follow its L bank over several feeder streams as the path swings gradually towards the S in a big curve down the Leisse valley. There are more marmots, and up amongst the rock outcrops and screes of la Grande Casse's SE flanks you might well see chamois and bouquetins. 1 kilometre beyond where the Vanoise stream falls opposite to join the Leisse, GR55 arrives at the

● 1h 30m – **PONT DE CROÉ-VIE** 2099m (6886ft) – *(20 mins S, Refuge d'Entre-Deux-Eaux, 60 places, guardian 15/6 to 25/9, all equipment, meals; path access S to GR5 at the Rocheure torrent).*

Cross the stone bridge R, over the Leisse and attack the zig-zag ascent of the steep slopes under Pointe de la Réchasse. Near the rocky ground towards the top, you pass a monument erected in memory of two army officers who died on the mountain, and soon arrive at an

● 45m – **ANCIENT BLOCKHOUSE** 2439m (8002ft).

Soon the trail veers L (WNW), crossing the Vanoise stream and following the R shore of a large marshy basin under extensive screes R. Continue to climb gently across stony terrain, passing along the SW banks of the Lac du Col de la Vanoise and the Lac Rond, reaching the

● 1h 15m – **REFUGE DU COL DE LA VANOISE** 2517m (8258ft) – 156 *places (36 when unguarded), guardian 15/6 to 15/9 and Easter, bedding and kitchen equipment, meals, extremely busy in season.*

From the col, GR55 follows the ancient glaciated valley of the Grande Casse, enclosed on both sides by steep slopes. Leave the refuge by a mule track N, past Lac Long, then W by zig-zags, descending down through rocks and across the marshy Lac des Vaches on large stones. Continue on down WSW, ignoring a path off R, cross a stream at a little bridge, pass some ruins L and arrive on the National Park boundary at

● 1h 15m – **CHALETS DE LA GLIÈRE** 2030m (6660ft) – *possible wild camping, nearby Refuge des Barmettes, 25 places, guardian mid-June to mid-Sept.*

The trail continues to descend, crossing the Glière torrent and passing beneath the Fontanettes téléski. At the fork soon after, keep L but ignore the next L turn which drops more steeply into the Glière valley. Keep to the R of the téléski, in and out of forest, all the way down to the road at

● 45m – **FONTANETTES** 1644m (5394ft) – *car parking.*

Turn R, then immediately L, cutting off a road bend, and at the next hairpin take a path down L, along the edge of trees, with the Glière below L. This emerges at a chapel and road at les Bieux, but carry on ahead through le Barioz and turn R into

● 20m – **PRALOGNAN-LA-VANOISE** 1418m (4652ft) – *all supplies, bars, cafes, restaurants, gîtes d'étape, Refuge de la Chévrerie, campsite, PTT, tourist information, car parking.*

Pralognan is a mountaineering and skiing centre of some note. During the first week of August each year there is a 'Cultural Week' with conferences, guided hiking tours on various themes, etc.

GR55 leaves the village by a street S, passing a campsite and turning R along the edge of the Isertan forest. Pass another small campsite L and a bridge R, proceed up through trees and past two more bridges over the Chavière. Thereafter, the trail climbs in forest above the torrent's L bank to the

● 45m – **PONT DE GERLON** 1592m (5223ft) – *possible wild camping.*

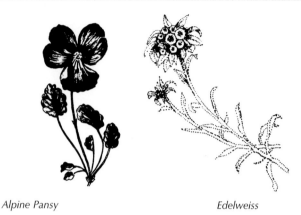

Alpine Pansy                                    Edelweiss

Cross the bridge and follow the track along the Chavière's W bank, beneath the precipitous slopes of Petit Mont Blanc. There are meadows here rich with wild flowers, and oats are still harvested. At le Prioux hamlet *(Refuge Le Repoju, 20 places, open July-Sept.)*, a bridge takes you to the torrent's E side, past parking space at les Ruelles, reaching

● 1h – **PONT DE LA PÊCHE** 1764m (5787ft).

GR55 crosses the Doron de Chavière torrent again and a few dozen metres upstream comes to the last trees (willow and birch) before the descent to Modane. It climbs up the valley, across unmown pastures containing many beautiful flowers, including the large Yellow Gentian. Pass on the R a path leading N to the Col du Mône and Petit Mont Blanc (2677m, 8783ft) and proceed S past the chalets of la Motte and Chapendu up to the L. At the Ritort oratory there is a path fork. GR55 takes the R branch, but the L branch leads, in 7 hours, over to the Arc valley via the Col d'Aussois (2916m, 9567ft), the Refuge du Fond d'Aussois (see GR5 route notes for details) and the GR5 at Plan d'Amont. This trail is more difficult than the normal GR5 standard.

At Ritort, note also the large cattle sheds and several acres of Alpine Sorrel. Around the rock-strewn little meadows, spring flowers push up through the snow, sprouting leaves and growing into bushy clumps later in the season.

Above the Arc valley, Stage 3

On the descent from Col de la Vallee Etroite, Stage 4

GR55 continues to climb steadily, SW then S, now in the Doron de Valpremont valley. It passes the chalets of Mollaret d'en bas and d'en haut above the torrent's rocky little gorge, swinging R to follow a feeder stream at la Rama chalet, turning S again to cross it and arriving by a path up across rocks R at the

● 2h 30m – **REFUGE DE PÉCLET-POLSET** 2474m (8117ft) – *80 places (30 in winter), guardian 15/6 to 15/9 plus Spring and bank holiday weekends, bedding equipment, gas stove, kitchen utensils, meals, toilets, washroom.*

(20 mins NW – easy ascent to the Lac Blanc in a spectacular setting. The trickles of water which feed the lake contain mineral deposits of many shades of red and white. Returning from the lake, a path just above the refuge, W then S through rocks, rejoins GR55 by a large pool.)

GR55 climbs S and crosses possible snowfields to reach the final and very steep approach to the

*Looking back to the Vanoise on the climb to the Col de Chavière*

● 1h 20m – **COL DE CHAVIÈRE** 2796m (9173ft) – *A magnificent high mountain location, with widespread views including all the principal Vanoise glaciers, Mont Blanc, Mont Pelvoux, the Ecrins, Mont Thabor and snow-covered peaks and ridges all round. The col is further distinguished by being the highest point reached on the GR5 trail.*

The path leaves the col R, then L down over eroded and shattered mountainside (follow the cairns carefully) to pass a rocky cirque L, holding the Lac de la Partie. Shortly after there is a

● 45m – **PATH JUNCTION** 2504m (8215ft).

(The L fork leads, in 2h 15m, to the Refuge de l'Orgère and D106 road (see GR5 route notes for details). This route is little frequented and offers the walker a chance to see numerous marmots, chamois (beneath the Râteau d'Aussois) and, with patience and good luck, bouquetins up towards the Aiguille Doran.)

The R fork continues GR55's descent, over le Grand Planay (sometimes you can see bouquetins amongst the rocky cliffs to the E), over a stream and into forest above the E bank of the St. Bernard stream. At the hamlet of Polset, follow a track down, short-cutting two bends, to the D106 road. Cross it and take a mule-track S to the L of a building near the

● 1h 40m – **RUISSEAU ST. BERNARD**.

Follow the GR5 route notes down to Modane.

# GR5E VARIANT

## From **PATH JUNCTION ABOVE BONNEVAL-SUR-ARC**

Continue ahead to the D902 road at a bridge, following it down for approximately 600 metres to a R bend. Watch here for a GR waymark at the start of a small path winding down a steep grassy hillside to cross the road again, pass down a track and enter

● 1h – **BONNEVAL-SUR-ARC** 1783m (5850ft) – *provisions, restaurants, hotels. Refuge Tralenta, 14 places, open all year, reservations essential. (Camping is not allowed in the commune territory of Bonneval and other Haute-Maurienne villages, except on designated campsites, of which there are a reasonable number. Much of the Arc valley is farmed, although lower down in the Arc forest there are more possibilities for discreet wild camping); tourist information, car parking, buses for the Arc valley and Modane.*

Bonneval is an archetypal Haute-Maurienne village, the only one in its original state, and has been preserved as a showpiece. In many ways this is admirable, but there are built-in contradictions. Bright, newly-varnished timber in the windows and doors of ancient buildings is visually jarring and the narrow streets are busy with us tourists, shopping for souvenirs in the surprisingly cosmopolitan shop interiors. Times have changed – a 16th-century French poet, Jaques du Mans, wrote,

> 'And Bonneval where the Arc has its spring,
> During the cold seasons your inhabitants
> Stay in their houses, cut off by winds and snow;
> And whole families, thus imprisoned,
> Live half the year on one batch of bread
> And the icicles round their windows
> Make a frame against the wind'.

Leave the village by forking R at a shrine, walking along the course of the old road on the Arc's R bank, with views ahead of snow-capped Pointe de Rouce. Over a torrent, the fields R are scattered with massive boulders from the mountainsides above. Pass stone sheds and beehives

*Bonneval-sur-Arc*

and, on a now narrow path, cross a stream and approach the 'Rocher de Château' – a cliff of black and white serpentine, reputed to contain prehistoric paintings (there are certainly rock-climbs judging by the abandoned slings!). Continue across flowery meadows with waterfalls cascading down the precipices opposite. The track passes crystal-clear ponds, crosses hayfields and joins a lane, turning R up to

● 1h 15m – **LE VILLARON** 1750m (5741ft) – *water, Gîte d'étape La Batisse, 36 places.*

The trail linking the Haute-Maurienne villages is called 'Sentier du Petit Bonheur' and waymarking, when it occurs, takes the form of wooden signposts rather than the familiar red and white stripes. In winter it is a popular cross-country ski route.

An unofficial route to Bessans exists along the Arc's R bank, but GR5E leaves by a track L at the top of the hamlet, zig-zagging up to a sign at the junction with GR5 coming down from the N. Turn L down by low cliffs to a broad riverside track, leading over a bridge to

● 45m – **BESSANS** 1705m (5594ft) – *provisions, bars, hotels, campsite (the actual site, Les Chardonettes, is near the river 2 kilometres W), PTT, tourist information, buses for the Arc valley and Modane, access to GR5.*

Wood carving made Bessans famous in the 18th century and pedlars flocked here to stock up on its bird-shaped boxes and its devils. In time of plague or famine during the Middle Ages, God and the Devil co-existed for the people of the Maurienne and effigies of the Devil can still be found in the village. There is an annual 'Saints and Devils' procession on August 15th. Its other symbol is St. Anthony, healer of sickness and watcher over the Evil One. A chapel dedicated to him rises above the village and contains some superb naive frescoes. Bessans was largely burned down by the Germans in 1944 and has been re-built in traditional Maurienne style.

GR5E takes a minor road W out of the village, crossing the Ribon torrent over Pont de Charriondaz. At the D902, take a track opposite, down through the campsite and beyond into delightfully scented forest. Follow signs ahead for Lanslevillard, climbing steadily above a gorge through which the Arc flows, unseen below. Crossing a torrent bed, the trail reaches the ancient Chantelouve d'en Bas chalets and a magnificent view W of la Dent Parrachée and the Arc valley. Descend the track, down zig-zags, over a bouldery torrent and take the R fork easily down to l'Envers and R into

● 2h 30m – **LANSLEVILLARD** 1500m (4921ft) – *provisions, hotels, campsite, tourist information, buses for Arc valley and Modane, path access NE up to GR5 at le Coin Bas.*

The village contains a chapel with many elaborate and rich frescoes dedicated to the 'Mystery of St. Sebastian' and well worth visiting.

From here W, the region is being developed as a winter ski resort and it is likely that the GR5E routing will change here and there as buildings sprout and pistes are cleared. Certainly, the section to Lanslebourg is rather short on quality.

Pass a chapel and crucifix, turning R down to a large church and L along the street, branching L at a road sign for Chambéry. Turn L up over a stream and down the field ahead, dropping down a bank to the course of a new road (likely to be re-routed). Turn L and proceed along the track to a holiday centre and thence to the N6 which crosses the Arc R and enters

● **45m – LANSLEBOURG-MONT-CENIS** 1400m (4594ft) – *all supplies, bars, cafes, restaurants, hotels, campsite, PTT, tourist information, buses for the Arc valley and Modane, path access N to GR5 at the Refuge de Cuchet.*

Since 1980, the Fréjus rail and road tunnel from Modane to Bardonecchia has turned the Maurienne into a link between the motorways of the Rhône and the Italian Po valley. Previously, all road traffic took the N6 over the Mont Cenis pass, but it is closed in winter. Lanslebourg straddles this main road which still takes a regular stream of tourist traffic and heavy lorries across into Italy during the summer months.

It is a surprise to find two churches facing each other at the W end of the town. The N one, dating from 1677, had three naves but the lateral one fell into ruin. After serving as town hall, Palace of Justice and school, the building is now designated as the 'Spiritual Centre of the Vanoise'.

If the town is not to be visited, keep to the Arc's L bank. From the town, re-cross the river on an iron-latticed bridge near a tannery, turning L then R up a forestry track and passing the campsite below R. Follow signs to Termignon, keeping well above the valley floor. Termignon is worth a detour to see its charming old domestic architecture and famous chapel and crucifix. When the forestry track becomes metalled, Termignon is sighted over a rise R (if the fields are not crop-filled, walk 100 metres R for good views of the communal open-field system above the village, leading up towards the jagged rock summit of la Dent Parrachée). Cutting off the lane hairpin, drop down to the remarkable wooden crucifix of St. Andrée and the simple chapel alongside. Walk over the bridge into

● **1h 30m – TERMIGNON** 1300m (4265ft) – *provisions, restaurants, hotels, Gîte d'étape La Para, 40 places, open all year, campsite, PTT, tourist information, buses for Arc valley and Modane, path access N to Refuge de l'Arpont and Montafia on GR5.*

GR5E leaves the village on a good track S, along the Arc's L bank through fields and past a campsite to reach the double village of

● 45m – **SOLLIÈRES-SARDIÈRES** 1300m (4265ft) – *campsite, path access N to Chalets de la Loza on GR5, archaeology exhibition at Sollières.*

The trail now follows a little-used minor road, past a small airfield L. The sense of being in more southerly regions of the Alps is now heightened as vegetation becomes drier and more thorny and hopping insects more abundant.

At a small quarry, fork up L, then R near le Chatel settlement. Soon Bramans is visible ahead. Keep L above new chalets on a popular forest track used for horse-riding (horses are kept in a paddock R) and descend through pine trees to a small campsite. Turn L, crossing a wide torrent on a plank bridge and arriving at

● 1h 30m – **BRAMANS** 1250m (4101ft) – *bar, hotel, Gîte/hotel Les Glaciers, 65 places, open all year except May and Nov., campsite, PTT, tourist information, buses for the Arc valley and Modane.*

Leave the village by a street down to the N6, along which turn L for about 1 kilometre. Take a track R, over the Arc and past an ancient quarry. The track climbs gradually, veering N up the small valley of the St. Pierre stream. After passing a cross mounted on a rocky bluff R, the trail crosses the stream and turns L into

● 1h – **AUSSOIS** 1483m (4865ft) – *hotels, campsite, tourist information.*

On a level with Aussois, the Maurienne valley contains a number of large fortifications – one of them ('Marie-Christine') is renovated. These forts were built in the 19th century by the king of Piémont-Sardaigne, as was, to defend his people against a possible French attack, and they are now a unique example of this type of mountain architecture.

Follow a road N from the village, turning off L before a téléski and climbing through Prédemal hamlet to the road again. Turn L along it for 1 kilometre and take a path off R at the bridge over the Benoit stream. Climb to the E end of the dam, where there are two alternatives. Either turn R and climb to GR5 at le Djoin téléski, or turn L over the dam and scale the steep E slopes leading to the GR5 traverse of the Col du Barbier. Thereafter, GR5 is followed to Modane.

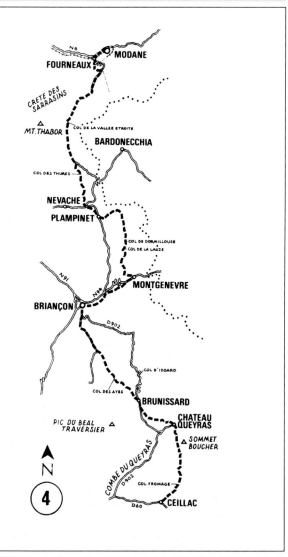

# STAGE FOUR

# *MODANE TO CEILLAC*

## 4–5 days

GR5 crosses the Hautes-Alpes and enters the Department of Alpes-de-Haute-Provence, with the weather growing drier and sunnier as continental and Mediterranean influences impinge.

The trail from Modane traverses impressively wild terrain into the Vallée Étroite, whose stream flows, via the Doire, into the Po at Turin. The Étroite valley was annexed by France in 1947 and the area, close to Italy's northern conurbation, still has an Italian flavour.

On a southward journey, the mountains seem gradually to have become less high and inhospitable. There are no glaciers, little permanent snow and vegetation is favoured on the gentler, sunny slopes. The Briançonnais region produces medicinal and herbal products from its plants and the Queyras Regional Park, around the river Guil, is widely known as 'alpine flower country'. Its forests contains a wide variety of species, from lower-altitude oak, ash, elm and maple to pine, beech and fir and the characteristic larch, which constitutes 60% of the total tree population and thrives up to 2200 metres. Larch, in fact, is ideally suited to the dry atmosphere; it can withstand cold well and some specimens live for several hundred years.

The stage is dominated by Briançon, ancient centre of a region rich in history and worth more than a fleeting visit. The cols of Ayes and Fromage are approached by long, shallow ascents through forest and meadow, yet their southern slopes are arid and stony from relentless exposure to strong sunlight and the effects of erosion.

**MODANE** 1066m (3497ft) – *all supplies, bars, cafes, restaurants, hotels, campsite, PTT, tourist information, buses for the Arc valley and Chambery, SNCF main line station.*

Walk SW along the N6, past the SNCF station L and into Fourneaux.

## PROFILE: STAGE 4
## MODANE TO CEILLAC

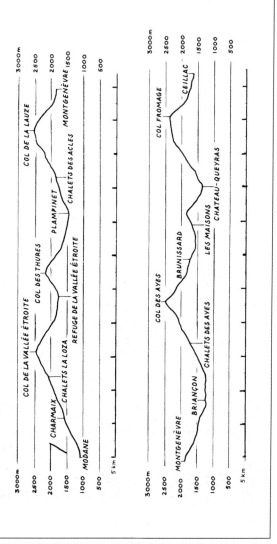

Pass the town hall and turn L. Cross the railway bridge and at a cross-road take the L turning, signposted 'Lanslebourg and Modane'. Bear R up past a modern church and over a gravelly level to a sign pointing R 'Charmaix 2 hrs'. Follow the stony track and look for the path ahead, under the road flyover, which climbs steadily through forest.

At a wide forestry track, turn L to a trail junction, whence the middle of three paths is followed, up then along, crossing three torrents. It becomes roughly motorable, leading out to new building development. A new road R passes under a ski-lift and reaches

● 2h – **CHARMAIX** 1572m (5157ft) – *small bar/restaurant, groceries, water.*

Cross the Ruisseau and follow its W bank past Les Herbiers hamlet. Further on, re-cross the stream to join an old military road leading to

● 1h 10m – **CHALETS LE LAVOIR** – *car parking, possible camping.*

The traverse of the Col de la Vallée Étroite is not steep and the terrain is easy in clear weather. However, there is little shelter in bad

*Pointe des Sarrasins (top left) and Roc Rouge (centre) above Modane*

conditions and the trail is not always clear on the ground, necessitating careful navigation in mist.

The path climbs more steeply SW to reach

● 30m – **CHALETS LA LOSA** 2099m (6886ft) – *path junction – R fork for GR54 'Tour de l'Oisans'; wild camping down by stream R.*

Waymarked occasionally on rocks, the trail now ascends grassy mountainsides up the valley's L flanks, past la Levette chalet, with widening retrospective views to the vast rocky summits and screes of the Sarrasins in the N. It is easy to expect to cross the Col de la Replanette, beckoning close on the L, but our col is still 3 kilometres distant to the SW.

Just before la Replanette (tiny stone shepherds huts), you can take one of two paths. The lower R fork is the official line, but the higher fork L is more pleasing, though not waymarked for 2 kilometres where the paths converge.

Cross screes beneath la Gringoil, through a lunar landscape of raw, eroded slopes and boulders, barren and desolate were it not for the covering of bright green lichens. The Combe de la Grande Montagne R, below le Mounioz and the Crête des Sarrasins in the N, is one of the most impressively wild (*sauvage* as the French would say) mountain settings on GR5.

(*A little before the col, a path off R leads, in 20 mins, to the Refuge de Thabor, 36 places, guardian July and Aug.*)

GR5 turns L (S) and reaches the

● 1h 20m – **COL DE LA VALLÉE ÉTROITE** 2434m (7985ft).

Situated on the ancient Franco-Italian border, the col is now on the dividing line between the Savoie and the Hautes-Alpes.

Descend in a southerly direction over thin turf, following the L bank of the Tavernette torrent and keeping R of a low hill. To the W rises the high bulk of Mont Thabor, 3178m (10,426ft). Cross the stream to a flatter, meadowy area on the R of the valley, over stony hillocks, then follow the path down, finally through conifers to

● 1h 30m – **PONT DE LA FONDERIE** 1897m (6224ft) – *rough road access, wild camping possible, water.*

*Refuge du Thabor (right of centre) with le Munioz behind,*
*from the Col de la Vallée Étroite*

(Path R (W) climbs Mt. Thabor via Prat du Plan, Vallon du Diner, the Chapelle Notre-Dame de Bon-Secours and the E ridge – allow a day for the ascent and descent.)

The motorable track leads SSE accompanied by the clear rushing waters of the Vallée Étroite torrent L. On fine weekends this is a popular picnic destination for Italian families (signs are in Italian too). Continue gently downhill to the

● 45m – **REFUGE DE LA VALLÉE ÉTROITE** 17765m (5790ft) – *40 places, guardian 20/6 to 20/9, bedding equipment, meals.*

The road S leads eventually to Bardonecchia, but GR5 turns R on a path zig-zagging steeply up through thin forest. During the ascent, look back to the vast, grey, tiered screes beneath Pointe Gaspard across the Étroite valley. The Franco-Italian frontier runs along the mountain crest. The trail bears L to cross the Mille valley, in and out of trees, finally climbing less steeply up to the almost circular little Lac Chavillon and over open pasture to the broad

● 1h 20m – **COL DES THURES** 2194m (7198ft) – *good views NE to the Rois Mages and N to the rocky towers of Séru and Thabor.*

GR5, now heading S, descends gently alongside the Thures stream to reach the

● 25m – **CHALETS DES THURES** 2106m (6909ft) – *water, possible wild camping.*

(Just after the chalets, there is a path junction. The L fork leads to Chapelle St-Roch, above Plampinet, on the **GR5B** variant offering excellent views of the Bardonecchia valley and frontier massifs. **Timings:** 1h – COL DE L'ECHELLE 1762m (5781ft); into Italy and back into France over the 2h 45m – COL DE PERTUSA 2228m (7310ft); 1h – CHAPELLE ST-ROCH 1846m (6056ft); rejoin GR5.)

GR5 takes the R fork, soon descending in zig-zags through old pine trees and by weird pillars of yellow rock. Ahead lie great scars on the hillsides where erosion has bared the underlying sedimentary rock. The trail crosses the Robion torrent (usually dry in summer) and the L bank of the small gorge is followed down to a forest road leading out to the valley of the river Clarée and

● 1h 30m – **CHAPELLE DES AMES** 1623m (5325ft).

Here, some decisions need to be taken! 15 mins W is le Cros hamlet *(some groceries and bread)* and the junction with the **GR5C** variant S to Briançon. This variant is for walkers with mountaineering experience and is not suitable in bad weather. **Timings:** 2h 45m – PORTE DE CRISTOL 2483m (8146ft); 45m – COL DE GRANON 2404m (7887ft); 20m – COL DE BARTEAUX 2382m (7815ft); 1h 45m – SERRE DES AIGLES 2567m (8422ft); 1h 25m – CROIX DE TOULOUSE 1962m (6437ft); rejoin GR5 at Briançon.

45 mins W is NÉVACHE – *cafe/restaurant, hotel, several gîtes d'étape, campsite, water, buses for Briançon.*

GR5 itself now continues ESE from Chapelle des Ames, through grassy fields alive with crickets, to the D994. Cross the Robion then turn L alongside the broad Clarée river before crossing it, too, at Pont des Armands. The old road from Névache is followed SE mostly in delightful pine forest with clearings, ideal for the camping it offers (official and unofficial). Rejoin D994 at a chapel just before the lovely

village of

1h – **PLAMPINET** 1482m (4862ft) – *bar, hotel, Gîte d'étape La Cleida (20 places, guardian all year, dormitory (sleeping bag necessary), situated next to a restaurant); camping (back in forest), buses for Briançon and Névache.*

*Plampinet*

GR5 leaves the village by a street N, then E on an ancient route, zig-zagging up and following the Acles torrent into its narrow gorge. After la Cléda blockhouse R, you reach Chapelle Saint-Roch and the path junction with GR5B from the NE. On flatter terrain, the trail soon reaches

● 1h 45m – **CHALETS DES ACLES** 1870m (6135ft) – *water, possible milk, no camping or fires.*

In a short while the trail narrows to a path and swings S round the Pointe de Pece, then crosses the Acles torrent on a small bridge before also crossing the l'Opon torrent and following it up. Above the tree line are rhododendrons, and past these GR5 mounts easily to the

● 1h 45m – **COL DE DORMILLOUSE** 2445m (8021ft).

From the col, the trail is clearly L (SE), climbing towards the Crête de la Lauze and the conspicuous

● 30m – **COL DE LA LAUZE** 2530m (8300ft).

Take the good path down E into the Clos des Fonds valley, soon joined by a path coming in from the N. The ground becomes less steep and there are springs (wild camping possible) before you pass through thin woods of larch. At about 2025m, near a ruin, join a stony track in the valley bottom and follow it down, under a téléski, to veer R and reach the D994. Turn R for 1 kilometre to enter, by its church, the town of

● 2h 10m – **MONTGENÈVRE** 1849m (6066ft) – *Gîte rural Le Cairn (5 rooms); provisions, bars, restaurants, hotels, campsite, PTT, bank (W at Les Albert hamlet), buses for Briançon and Chaviéres.*

Favoured by good snowfall, long hours of sunshine and by being near the only road col in the French Alps open all winter, Montgenèvre has been an important winter sports resort since before the Second World War. Long before that, the armies of Caesar, Charlemagne, Charles VIII and Napoleon had used the col, Napoleon's armies having constructed the first road.

Leave the town SW along N94 for over 1 kilometre. Watch L for a turning down across a tiny wooden bridge over the Durance and follow the path above its L bank, reaching an irrigation canal along which the trail continues for 1½ kilometres in the Bios des Bans forest (possible wild camping). Turn R on a path down over a torrent bed, leading out to the forest edge by a cross and R onto a track. This passes in front of a ruined chapel just before la Vachette. Turn L into more woods, reaching a dry diverted-water channel which is followed then crossed. With the Durance below R, the trail comes to the Serre-Boyer ravine, prone to landslip. There are good views ahead to the Pont d'Asteld and old Briançon perched on its hilltop. 500 metres further on there is a

● 2h – **PATH JUNCTION** 1340m (4396ft).

To by-pass Briançon fork L on **GR5D** via Font-Christine and – 20 mins – PONT DE CERVIÉRE: turn SE then sharply W after 2½ kilometres down to 50 min – SACHAS 1240m (4068ft); rejoin GR5.

*Briançon*

The R fork – GR5 – descends to **le FONTEUIL**; in the village is a *gîte d'étape*. The route continues up past fascinating sundials into

● 30m – **BRIANÇON** 1290m (4232ft) – *all supplies, bars, cafes, restaurants, hotels, campsite, PTT, tourist office, bank, doctor/pharmacy, buses for Gap, Grenoble, Clavières and Champéry; SNCF (end of line up Rhône valley – trains direct for Marseilles).*

The highest city of its size in France, and second only in altitude in the whole of Europe to Davos, Switzerland, Briançon occupies a unique position. It lies like the hub of a huge wheel whose spokes are easily accessible valleys and tracks of great antiquity. As well as being partly industrial and an administrative and commercial centre, Briançon is rich in history, and the citadel-like layout of the old town attracts many thousands of tourists. The fortifications, barracks and emplacements built around natural features bear witness to an impressive investment in defence. From 1713, the town was the guardian of the strategically important Col de Montgenèvre and in 1913 the military garrison of 4000 men outnumbered the civilian population (with profitable repercussions for the town's economy).

Today the garrison is much smaller and trains troops in mountain warfare.

To rejoin GR5 at Sachas, leave the town S, past the railway station, either turning L to Pont de Cervières (see GR5D notes above) or continuing on the D36 towards Villard-St-Pancrace. *(Gîte Le Bois de Baracan, 40 places, open all year.)*

GR5 waymarks now lead walkers on an undulating valley course, before reaching Soubeyran, turning L and passing the Chapelle Saint-Laurent. The trail now zig-zags S up into the Grand Bois du Villard and climbs along stony, pine-covered slopes above the W bank of the Ayes torrent. Further on, cross the torrent and pass the St. Elizabeth chapel at the settlement of

● 1h 30m – **CHALETS DES AYES** 1711m (5613ft) – *water, milk, possible wild camping, road access and car parking space.*

Keep L of the hamlet with its school camp, taking a path SE besides the Ayes. Avalanches have left trails of destruction through the forest in places and the path is likely to be re-routed. Arrive over grassy slopes at

● 1h 20m – **CHALETS DE VERS LE COL** 2163m (7096ft) – *possible wild camping.*

Hereabouts the trail enters the Queyras Regional Park, created in 1977 to protect and promote interest in the flora and fauna, local crafts, forests, etc.

GR5 concludes its long ascent SE, climbing steadily across rough pasture with impressive cliffs and screes L under the Crête de Burguet, up to the

● 45m – **COL DES AYES** 2477m (8126ft) – *once a busy thoroughfare between Briançon and Queyras.*

The trail's overall SE direction is maintained off the col, first down zig-zags then over several clear streams amidst clouds of butterflies and past the l'Eychaillon chalets (2142m). There is an acute bend N in the track to round the warm-coloured cliffs of Crête de l'Apaliar, more descending zig-zags, then a straighter section above the L bank of the Rivière torrent, through stunted conifers *(rough road access and car parking space)*. (Just before reaching the D902, which climbs tortuously

*High mountain pasture above Château Queyras*

to the N over Col d'Izoard, there is a path off L (N) for the GR58 'Tour du Queyras'.) You now cross small fields, keeping R of the buildings at

● 2h – **BRUNISSARD** 1746m (5728ft) – *provisions, bar/cafe, possible shelter, Gîte d'étape Auberge des Bon Enfants, 24 places, meals, showers.*

Walk down the road, perhaps commiserating with sweating cyclists facing the long Izoard ascent, to reach

● 20m – **LA CHALP** 1685m (5528ft) – *water, Gîte d'étape La Teppio, souvenirs (especially local wood carvings), bar/cafe.*

Waymarking points GR5 walkers on down the road (25 mins) to Arvieux, presumably to tempt them with the village amenities – *supplies, hotel/restaurant.* Welcome though all this may be, it does involve the walker in a subsequent ascent of over 100 metres and 1½ kilometres up the D502 to rejoin GR5.

The official line passes along the L edge of la Chalp, bearing gently R to climb gradually through trees along the valley's E flank, crossing the Glaisette and Pellas torrents and arriving at the ancient barns of

● 45m – **LES MAISONS** 1693m (5554ft).

The trail climbs steadily past fields and grassy banks alive, on a hot day, with crickets and grasshoppers. There is a path junction L – GR58 ' Tour du Queyras'.

*(45 mins N – Gîte de Souliers, 60 places, guardian all year, bedding and kitchen equipment, meals.)*

Forest is entered on a virtual plateau and you come soon to the man-made Lac de Roue (possible wild camping). Thereafter begins the long descent to Château Queyras, first over gentle slopes then down more steeply on a rough path with the fort below framed by conifers. At the D947, turn L on a dangerous little 500m road dash along to

● 1h 45m – **CHÂTEAU QUEYRAS** 1350m (4429ft) – *provisions, restaurant, hotels, barn accommodation ('La Halte du Randonneur') with shower and toilet, campsite, buses for Abriès and Montdauphin/Guillestre (SNCF).*

The rock outcrop dominating the valley was probably used by early man for defensive purposes, but we do know that the present fortifications were constructed in 1700. The small town is in two parts – one built round the fort, the other on the N bank of the Guil.

GR5 leaves S, to the E of the fort, over the Guil and steeply up through pine forest. At the minor road (leading up to Sommet Bucher), turn L, round a hairpin, taking a path off R at the next sharp bend. At the road again, walk along it a short distance before taking the path R off the bend, near barracks. Do not follow the wider track close to the Bramousse torrent's L bank, but climb gradually SSE and watch for GR waymarks on a narrow path winding up through meadows, more or less parallel to the torrent. A track joins from the L (from the Col des Prés-de-Fromage) then you cross the Bramousse R and in about 1 kilometre the trail turns sharp R (NW). It climbs to spot-height 2263m before resuming its S direction. There are panoramic views to the NW, back along the route, and the mountains are scrub-covered and barren compared to the luxuriance of the Northern Alps.

The trail undulates pleasantly S, past huge eroded gullies R, over coarse scree slopes and rises gradually to the grassy

● 3h 45m – **COL FROMAGE** 2301m (7549ft) – *possible shelter 100m E of col in dilapidated concrete hut.*

*Château Queyras*

Ignoring a path R under the Crête des Chambretta, descend S down zig-zags on the R of the Rassis ravine and over stony ground to a cart track at le Villard. Turn R above a cross, taking a path L to emerge on a road following the Cristillian river and which leads down to

● 1h 30m – **CEILLAC** 1639m (5377ft) – *all supplies (the last before Larche), bars, cafes, restaurants, Gîte d'étape Les Baladins (70 places, 20 in winter, guardian all year, bedding and kitchen equipment, showers, meals possible during summer, in village during winter); hotels, campsite, PTT, telephone, buses for Montdauphin, access to GR58 'Tour de Queyras'.*

## STAGE FIVE

# CEILLAC TO ST. ETIENNE-DE-TINÉE

### 4 days

The traverse of the Hautes-Alpes takes GR5 over its highest cols (apart from Isèran): Giradin and Pas de la Cavale. There may be no permanent snow, but this is lofty, remote country which deserves to be taken seriously. The terrain is often rough and stony, gradients sometimes very steep and usually lengthy, but for the well-prepared walker the rewards are considerable. Some of the most stunning high-mountain scenery on the entire GR5 is to be found in this stage.

From Ceillac, the trail rises acutely at first through forest, past the exquisite turquoise Sebeyrand and St. Anne lakes, the latter with its tiny chapel surrounded by high rocky mountainsides. Crossing the exciting Col Giradin, we descend into the remote Ubaye valley and follow a narrow road down, over the sensational Pont Châtelet, to Fouillouze. The Vallonnet and Mallemort cols follow and take us past old wartime buildings down to the small border town of Larche, rebuilt after its destruction in 1944 by the occupying forces. Here begins the ascent, up the Lauzanier valley nature reserve, of the final major mountain barrier to be crossed – the rugged and less-frequented Pas de la Cavale. There is a magnificent panorama of the Alpes-Maritimes ahead from the steep, rocky col.

Over three lower passes, GR5 then leads down to St. Dalmas-le-Selvage and thence to St. Etienne-de-Tinée, the Tinée valley pointing like a finger to the Mediterranean coast.

Ceillac is a year-round resort, situated at the confluence of the Cristillian and Mélezet rivers. It has an interesting old church and crucifix and its original character as a small farming community is still strongly evident, despite some new building development. GR5 leaves the village by an alleyway L of the town hall, crosses the Cristillian and proceeds SE along the road. After 2 kilometres (1¼ miles) and past the campsite, opposite the Hotel de la Cascade, GR5 turns R to cross the torrent over a wooden bridge. It then climbs very steeply to the R of the aptly named la Pisse waterfall, rising in cunning bends up what had looked from the valley floor to be unscalable rock walls.

The trail winds on up, protected here and there with handrails and entering woods. The zig-zags are numerous, with few let-ups, but a slow, steady pace enables a rhythm to be established. After crossing another footbridge at a small ravine, the path follows the torrent up. It splashes prettily down its rocky bed and, at the exit from the forest, is crossed again to reach the

● **2h – LAC DES PRÉS-SÉBEYRAND** 2287m (7503ft) – *possible wild camping.*

The Crête des Veyres is an immensely impressive barrier of jagged grey rock rising above skirts of scree ahead R. Keeping E of the lake, descend through a large depression and emerge onto a barren piste under a téléski. Follow this up until 100m short of the top station, there branching slightly L over boulders to reach an almost level area and the

● **1h 30m – CHAPELLE AND LAC SAINTE-ANNE** 2415m (7923ft) – *path NE (approx. 45 mins) down to roadhead in Mélezet valley.*

In a wild and beautiful setting, the turquoise lake has little sandy beaches and lies beneath a cirque of towering grey, snow-patched cliffs – the Pic des Heuvières, Pics de la Font Sancte (3385m, 11,105ft) and Tête de la Petite Part. The tiny chapel is the scene of an annual pilgrimage in traditional costume by the inhabitants of Ceillac and nearby Maurin each year on July 26th.

Leave the lake at its NE corner, aiming SE over thin grassy slopes and past rocky outcrops. The view back over the lake, Ceillac and across range upon range of sand-coloured mountains into the blue distance is breathtaking. The col can be seen clearly ahead and as it is approached you traverse more rocky ground, finally climbing steepish, fine scree by somewhat precarious zig-zags to reach the

● **1h – COL GIRADIN** 2700m (8858ft) – *Departmental border between the Hautes-Alpes and the Alpes-de-Haute-Provence.*

Ahead, across the deep trench of the Ubaye valley, there is the magnificent sight of the peaks of the Aiguille Pierre André and the

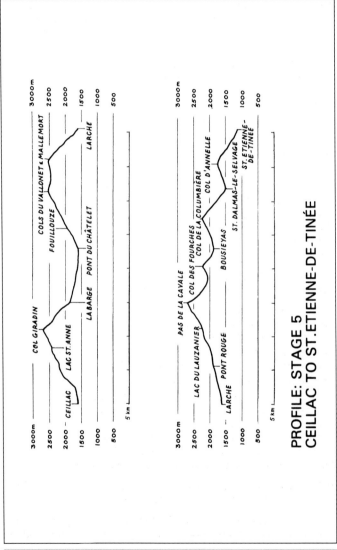

PROFILE: STAGE 5
CEILLAC TO ST.ETIENNE-DE-TINÉE

*Lac Sainte-Anne above Ceillac and a retrospective view
of the Hautes-Alpes*

Aiguille de Chambeyron.

From the little saddle with its wooden sign, drop down SE through boulders, first by zig-zags then following the bed of the Séchoirs torrent, past a tiny shepherd's hut R. At a spot-height 2380m, cross the dry bed, turning R and climbing a little.

*(A steep and rough path L (SE) leads, in 50 mins, to the Gîte (or Refuge) de Maljasset, 58 places, guardian all year except second and third weeks in May and the second fortnights in November and January, bedding and kitchen equipment, meals and drinks. Gîte La Cure, 30 places, open school holidays.)*

GR5 continues SW on a very thin path above high cliffs and is quite exposed for a short section. Thereafter it descends relentlessly and fairly steeply towards the hamlet whose rooftops are visible below. At the D25 road, turn R and enter

● 1h 50m – **LA BARGE** 1877m (6158ft) – *20 mins L, Gîte de Maljasset, mentioned above.*

GR5 uses the road SW for about 8 kilometres (5 miles). It is a favourite picnic area with French motorists, who can be observed lying on sunbeds, sitting at camp tables and playing boules while you plod steadfastly past them down the valley! At one point the old road through a tunnel is replaced by a new bridge crossing to the W bank, with views L up to the vertical faces and spires of la Berche de la Souvagea. To your R are red, green and yellow tinted rocks on the Grande-Caire. Pass the Chapelle Saint-Antonie L, cross the Châtelet torrent R and contour round the massive Châtelet rock which plugs the valley and carries the ruins of a château. Soon after, there is a

● 2h – **ROAD JUNCTION** 1625m (5331ft) – *(20 mins SW on D25 – Grande Serenne, hotel/restaurant, campsite. 45 mins SW on D25 – St. Paul-sur-Ubaye, supplies, bar, hotel, restaurant, PTT, public baths!)*

Turn L, across the Châtelet bridge (sensational 100m drop), pass through road tunnels, ascend dog-legs and arrive in

● 1h – **FOUILLOUZE** 1907m (6256ft) – *water, Gîte de Fouillouze (57 places, closed late May/early June and Dec., bedding and kitchen equipment, meals), car parking, path junction with GR6 'Alpes-Ocean', also GR56 'Tour de l'Ubaye' which heads W to St. Paul-sur-Ubaye.*

GR5 and GR56 leave the village by its chapel on a broad track SE, climbing through a scattering of larch above the L bank of the Fouillouze torrent. Pass the ruins of the Plate Lombard fort, cross two streams and climb above the last of the trees. Keeping generally SE, the trail ascends onto the flat and barren Plate Lombard before reaching the foot of a stiffer climb incorporating a big bend, between the Lac de Lombarde R and the distinctive shape of the Tête de Plate Lombarde L, to arrive at the

● 2h – **COL DU VALLONNET** 2524m (8281ft).

The ensuing descent is gradual, passing several springs and keeping E of the Grande lac du Vallonnet. Traverse a minor col and descend about 50m (160ft) SE to reach a level area. Without losing height, the trail circles round the Ravine du Pinet then contours the NW and W slopes beneath la Meyna. At some ruined barracks you are on a stony track, along which you veer R (W) then S to cross the

● 1h 15m – **COL DE MALLEMORT** 2558m (8392ft).

*Looking south-east from Col Giradin to the Aiguille de Chambeyron*

Descend to the S quite steeply, crossing a small valley. Around the 2100m (6890ft) level, after some zig-zags, vegetation has all but obscured the path in places. Keep SW at first, then SE, down the line of the broad ridge over grass, gradually bearing S to pass the ruins of Columbier farm, and join a path coming down from the NE in the Rouchouse valley, which you follow to

● 2h – **LARCHE** – 1670m (5479ft) – *provisions, hotels, restaurant, Gîte de Larche (45 places, guardian 15/6 to 15/11 and 15/12 to 30/5, bedding and kitchen equipment, meals), PTT, buses to Barcelonette then to Gap (SNFC), campsite.*

The town has been rebuilt after its destruction in August 1944 by the occupying forces and straddles the N100 road over the Col de Larche into Italy.

Turn off the main road E onto a minor one alongside the N bank of the Ubayette, crossing to the S bank after the Malboisset ruins. Continue SE, over le Pis stream, past a dry-stone shack and follow the road round S to the

● 1h 20m – **PONT ROUGE** 1907m (6256ft) – *wild camping, small shelter, car parking space.*

The wooden bridge announces entry to the beautiful Lauzanier valley, a nature reserve of some 3000 hectares created in 1935. Beyond the bridge, the road deteriorates but is still motorable for one or two kilometres.

The crossing of the Pas de la Cavale is a particularly rugged one, over remote terrain, and demands to be taken seriously. In bad weather, route-finding is not straightforward and there is a danger from stonefall in windy conditions on the descent. In good weather, however, it is a marvellous ascent in wild mountain scenery and views are exceptional.

GR5 follows the Ubayette up S, passing three separate little cabins, occupied in summer, and a wooden footbridge L before climbing up across the Lauze ravine (good clear streams) to the Donadieu cabin, a sheepfold and stone building with metal roof. Cross the Pradon ravine, past a ruin R. Beyond a little chapel the trail climbs to the

● 1h 40m – **LAC DU LAUZANIER** 2284m (7493ft) – *wild camping, water near shepherd's hut.*

Pass round the lake's W shore and climb S through a rugged and chaotic passage over rocks and boulders, cross a stream L and follow its E bank up to the Lac de Derrière la Croix. The lake lies at the N end of a vast basin, hemmed in on the W by the Tête de Pelouse, on the E by the Rochers des Trois Evêques and ahead (S) by the ridge wall we are about to cross. The trail swings in a big and unexpected loop to the L (E) up zig-zags and more small lakes become visible below. Good wild camping, but every sound echoes eerily round the encircling cliffs and the situation is as remote as any on GR5. Soon the path traverses steeper, stony slopes and is itself composed of large fragments which make walking a slow and patient process. Due S, it eventually arrives at the

● 1h 25m – **PAS DE LA CAVALE** 2671m (8763ft) – *situated on the border between the Alpes-de-Haute-Provence and the Alpes-Maritimes.*

Italy lies down to the L (E), beyond the rocky corner of the Trois Evêques, and to the SW the Alpes-Maritimes stretch green and inviting towards the Mediterranean, only 60 kilometres (37 miles) distant as the crow flies!

The S side of the col is extremely steep and once the initial path waymark has been located, care is needed descending the zig-zags over loose scree and around rocks. (If the 'Lombarde' wind is blowing hard from Italy, it is possible for loose stones to fall from the ridge above, with unpredictable consequences!)

The gradient gradually eases and the trail winds down onto grassier hillside and arrives at the

● 40m – **LACS D'AGNEL** 2343m (7687ft) – *wild camping.*

Looking back to the col over 300m (1000ft) above, it is hard to imagine how a walking route could have traversed the great grey bastion of jagged rock.

Pass the small lakes to the E and follow down the L bank of the Gypière combe. Soon you join a track coming down from the NE (Col de Pouriac), staying on it for about 200m before crossing the Gypière R to reach the mostly ruined barns of

● 30m – **SALSE MORÈNE** 2087m (6847ft).

Proceed SW then W to cross a channel, whereafter the trail is poorly waymarked as you pass a rough cabin (possible shelter) and cross the ravine leading down SE from the Castel de la Tour. Resuming a SW direction, climb to the head of a small valley and up to the

● 35m – **COL DES FOURCHES** 2262m (7421ft).

Take the earth track W to cross the D64 road near a monument. Descend and cross the road at a bend, and when you reach it again, walk along R for about 50 metres. Pass a sheepfold (spring above) and leave the road to descend the small Morade ravine (usually dry) before cutting the road twice more at the E corners of dog-legs. The trail then passes a former refuge to cross the D64 yet again and drop down to

● 45m – **BOUSIÉYAS** 1883m (6178ft) – *hotel/restaurant (no supplies or buses), Gîte de Bousiéyas (16 places summer and winter, guardian 15/6 to 15/9, bedding and kitchen equipment), telephone.*

Leave the hamlet W along the road and, round the first hairpin, look for the track off R, over the Tinée. It swings SE, crosses a small stream, then detours S, uphill, in a big 'V' to negotiate a large combe, becoming level for a while before climbing above forest round the

*The rugged slopes of Pic des Heuvières (top right),
Alpes-de-Haute-Provence*

Rocher du Prêtre. Generally SE, the trail traverses the upper Issias valley and, by zig-zags, reaches the

● **1h 15m – COL DE LA COLUMBIÈRE** 2237m (7339ft) – *path junction with GR56 'Tour de l'Ubaye'.*

(30 mins ENE leads by a good path up to the Tête de Vinaigre 2394m (7854ft). There are good views over the Tinée valley, and a military building on the summit.)

From the col descend zig-zags and contour round the E side of la Combe valley, passing above the ruined Coimain hut and dropping past barns at Rochepin. The trail veers NW to cross the valley bottom then SW down hillside into

● **1h 50m – ST. DALMAS-LE-SELVAGE** 1500m (4921ft) – *provisions, hotel/restaurants, Gîte d'étape (20 places, open all year); water, telephone, car parking, (daily shuttle buses to St. Etienne-de-Tinée).*

A picturesque mountain village at the confluence of the Sestrière and Jalorgues torrents, St. Dalmas is the venue for several summer fêtes. At its lower end is a church with an interesting Romanesque steeple.

Pass to the R of the church and proceed on a partly motorable track ESE over small torrents, in and out of forest, up to the

● **1h – COL D'ANELLE** 1739m (5705ft) – *car parking space.*

Turn L round a hillock and follow the clear forest track SE watching for where the path leaves R. Out of the trees, it's level walking past barns, with views R of the massively eroded grey gullies beneath the Crête du Content. Ahead, excitingly, lies the whale-back summit ridge of Mont Mounier, last sizeable mountain before the coast.

Where the path turns sharp R by two ruined barns, there are more superb views down the Tinée valley 600 metres (2000ft) below. Descend first through scattered pines, then past small fields, with the scent of wild lavender in the air. The old sunken path crosses a stony track *(car parking space)* and emerges at the huge, pink-stoned Jean Franco College. Follow signs for the hospital, aiming for the church spire near the centre of

● **1h 10m – ST. ETIENNE-DE-TINÉE** 1144m (3753ft) – *all supplies, bars, cafes, restaurants, hotels, campsite, Gîte d'étape (20 places, open all year); PTT, tourist information, hospital/pharmacy, buses for Auron and Nice via the Tinée valley, police station.*

Looking back to Col Giradin (centre right), Stage 5

# STAGE SIX

## ST. ETIENNE-DE-TINÉE TO NICE

### 5–6 days

The final stage on the southward trek is statistically and psychologically downhill but holds on resolutely to the spirit of a mountain route. The trail passes through the modern ski resort of Auron, traverses the Col du Blainon and descends across flowery, terraced hillsides dotted with ancient barns to the mountain hamlet of Roya. In the Mercantour National Park, opened against much opposition in 1979, GR5 climbs near to the summit of Mont Mounier where, for the first time, there are views S to the Mediterranean. Dropping through the curious village of Roure, we arrive at St. Sauveur-sur-Tinée, lowest point above sea level since Landry in the Isère valley.

St. Dalmas-Valdeblore is at the N end of a long limestone ridge running down to Utelle and heralds the final transition to the Mediterranean hinterland of Provence. St. Dalmas is also the departure point for the GR52 variant which swings N then E and S through remote and high mountain country to end at Menton on the coast not far from the Italian border. Throughout this last section on GR5 and GR52, water and accommodation become scarce and thunderstorms common during July and August, when temperatures can reach very high values.

Crossing the Vesubie gorge, GR5 passes olive terraces at Levens, contours Mont Cima and leads to Aspremont, built high above the Var plain on its little round hill. Mont Chauve d'Aspremont is the last high ground before GR5 descends through the suburbs then the city centre of cosmopolitan Nice and arrives at the Mediterranean shore.

Leave St. Etienne-de-Tinée by the Rue Droite behind the information centre, past the Gendarmerie and fork R at a crucifix and water trough. The lane becomes a rough track and further along you cross a stream and climb to the D39 road. Turn L and follow it for 300m then turn R up waymarked steps and onto a broad track up through forest.

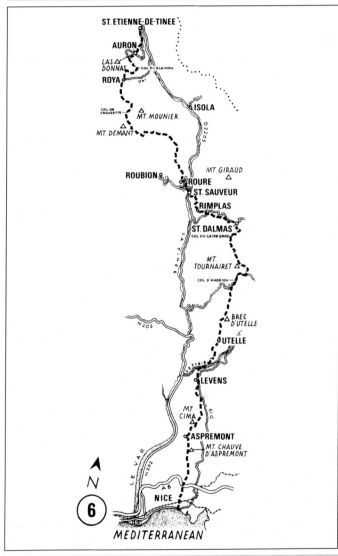

Narrowing to a path, the trail turns R and zig-zags rather uninterestingly up to a plateau at Collet. Follow the Chemin de Demandols S into

● 2h – **AURON** 1602m (5256ft) – *all supplies, bars, restaurants, hotels, campsite, PTT, tourist information, buses for St. Etienne and Nice, car parking.*

(Summer téléphérique to las Donnas 2256m (7401ft) – possible to rejoin GR5 at Col du Blainon.)

Auron is one of the new generation of year-round resorts, though it is principally one of the Alpes-Maritimes premier ski centres. Its brash, modern chalet architecture is in stark contrast to the mellow old buildings in St. Etienne, where even the pastel colours of exterior paintwork seem to have been harmonised by an unconscious consensus.

Cross the D39, cutting off a big dog-leg bend. Rejoining the road higher up, walk beneath the Las Donnas cable car and pass a chalet with water trough. Entering forest, the trail crosses the Blainon stream and winds uphill to reach

● 1h 15m – **COL DU BLAINON** 2011m (6598ft).

There is an excellent panorama ahead to Mont Mounier and back to the Pas de la Cavale.

Descend SW then S, past a ruined barn. The trail wanders gently down through meadows, past the ruinous St. Sebastian chapel. On these south-facing hillsides there are abundant wild flowers and herbs, marmots too. The imposing rocky summit of las Donnas rears ahead. The hillsides have been terraced and are scattered with barns built into the slope – some of the most beautiful on GR5.

Cross the Lugière torrent's bed and proceed up between two barns. The route then winds down past more barns and soon a small cluster of buildings and church are visible below. Cross a metalled lane, down a stony path and walk into the mountain hamlet of

● 1h 10m – **ROYA** 1500m (4921ft) – *water, bar/inn, Gîte de Roya (32 places, guardian in summer); unofficial camping, telephone, road access to the Tinée valley (buses for St. Etienne and Nice).*

Pass to the R of the church, down over the Roya torrent *(possible lightweight camping on grassy levels)*. Here GR5 enters the Mercantour

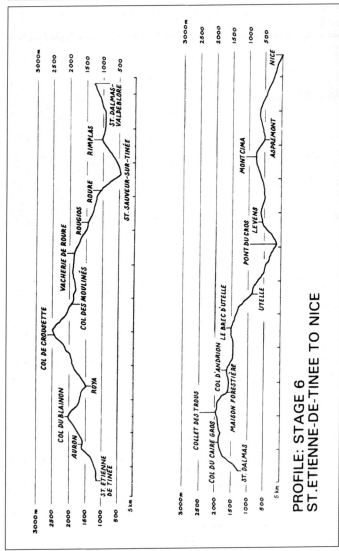

PROFILE: STAGE 6
ST. ETIENNE-DE-TINEE TO NICE

*The mountain hamlet of Roya*

National Park (note camping restrictions on board). Turn L over the Sellevieille torrent, mounting along its L bank to wind up through thin forest into a little gorge with orange cliffs, a waterfall and many aromatic plants and herbs. The trail emerges onto open, rocky ground to cross the Sellevieille torrent R (no bridge). Climb across mountainside, over a stream and pass a shepherd's hut before traversing L (E) round the valley head, zig-zagging up the shattered L end of the Barre de Sellevieille cliffs. GR5 now turns R (S) over the flatter, hillocky terrain in the Combe de Crousette *(water, wild camping, possible shelter in barn to W)* before finally climbing L of a low ridge more steeply up to the

- 3h 45m – **COL DE CROUSETTE** 2480m (8136ft).

Take the path L (SE), still climbing across Mont Mounier's flanks, to Stele Valette, the apex of three ridges. (A path leads N then veers NE, in 45 mins, to the ruined CAF refuge on Petit Mont Mounier. From there the summit ridge NE can be climbed straightforwardly in 30 mins to Mont Mounier, 2817m (9242ft). In clear weather it is possible, for the first time on the trek south, to see the Mediterranean – and, if you are particularly fortunate, Corsica too!)

GR5 descends SE from Stele Valette (after a short N turn), passing the Baisse du Demant and contouring the rough slopes of Mont Demant. Once beyond the Barre du Demant cliffs which bisect the valley L, the trail drops rapidly, still SE, to the Col du Refuge. Proceeding down E below the small summit of Mont des Moulines you round a stream head across stony ground and arrive at the

● 1h 30m – **COL DE MULINÉS** 1982m (6502ft) – *(Path S, yellow waymarks, leads in 1h 15m to BEUIL – provisions, hotels/restaurants, buses for Nice and Valberg).*

From the col, the trail descends L (NW) to cross the Demant stream, veers NE again in zig-zags on a better track to the L of the Pierre du Demant and crosses the Combe Maure valley. Leave the track for a less distinct path L, above Vignols hamlet, in and out of the Gourgette valley over loose ground and up through rocky outcrops to les Portes de Longon plateau (wild camping). Continue ESE, along the R bank of the Longon stream, to reach Roure cowshed, now converted into the

● 1h 35m – **GÎTE DE LONGON** – 1883m (6178ft) *20 places, guardian 20/6 to 20/9, meals, water, milk, cheese, exit from the Mercantour Park.*

There are waterfalls before the path, having followed the Longon's L bank down sharp bends, now crosses the stream on a little bridge and drops into forest, losing height quickly. You cross the spine of the Autcellier ridge and cross the l'Arcane stream to arrive at a large, mainly flat clearing in the forested mountainside, known as

● 1h 10m – **ROUGIOS** 1467m (4813ft) – *possible shelter in barns, water, wild camping.*

Many of the barns are derelict and the area doesn't seem to be worked much, though at one time it must have been a busy focus of farming activity. Wild camping is possible near a stream at the S forest edge, after which take care to turn R into la Frache forest itself, in which the path contours pleasantly round, past ruined barns and out onto open ground. There are plunging views into the Tinée valley and to the E lie the rocky summits of the Italian frontier massifs.

Descend the open slopes through aromatic plants and hopping insects, watching for lizards, down alongside irrigation channels to a tarred lane. Turn R, and round a hairpin take the path off R by a little fenced arena. Go down past the St. Sebastian chapel (marvellous 16th-century frescoes and gargoyles) and after the next road bend, look for an unmarked path by an electricity sub-station dropping to a large church at

● **1h 15m – ROURE** 1096m (3596ft) – *provisions, bar, Gîte de Roure (20 places, guardian all year, mattresses, blankets, kitchen equipment, showers, toilet, cold water), hotel, water, telephone, car parking, space, buses for St. Sauveur-sur-Tinée.*

This curious and charming little village, perched high above the Tinée valley, has lost more than half its population in the last 120 years and there seem to be few young people there now.

From the church, turn sharp L down a paved alley, through the tiny village square opposite arched water troughs. Continue down past houses, turning R for 150 metres at the road then off R at a hair-pin. Hereafter, the ancient path zig-zags delightfully down semi-cultivated hillside, with aerial views to the valley, crossing the road several times and arriving at a bridge over the Tinée just below

● **1h – ST. SAUVEUR-SUR-TINÉE** 496m (1627ft) – *provisions, bars, hotel/restaurants, Gîte de St. Sauveur-sur-Tinée (18 places, open May to Oct.), camping (turn L upstream, past tennis courts), PTT, buses for St. Etienne and Nice.*

St. Sauveur is the main market town of the mid-Tinée valley and retains its traditional spirit and identity despite being a popular sight-seeing and hiking destination.

At the village's S end, take a lane up L off the D2205, leaving it at the first bend for a path R, up past a lane bend to the St. Roch chapel. Continue to a TV booster station and turn L along the ancient track connecting the high villages of the Valdeblore. It narrows to a path, climbing pleasantly through deciduous forest. You pass a small vine-yard L and continue up the track, blasted dramatically from the shaley hillside. There are good views back to Roure and Mont Mounier. The trail rounds a bend and enters

● **1h 30m – RIMPLAS** 1016m (3333ft) – *water, bar, telephone, car parking.*

Rimplas sits on a little col and is built round alleyways and intimate squares, well worth exploring.

*St. Sauveur-sur-Tinée*

Follow the small road through the village and after a chapel L, take a path down R across dry, southern slopes covered with thorny vegetation, with lizards on rocks and walls, At a track, turn L past buildings, cross a stream and join the road for 200 metres, turning off L at a hairpin. The ancient paved track climbs through more deciduous woods to a lane-end where you carry on R to meet the road near a large church.

(500 metres half-left is LA BOLLINE – *provisions, hotel, water, PTT, buses for Nice.*)

GR5 turns R, however, onto the road, R again at the junction then immediately L up a tarred lane. This becomes a path and reaches another lane. Turn R, below la Roche village, up past new chalets, sharp L then R onto D2565 and in 50 metres down a lane R. Take the track L to short-cut the ascending road, finally turning R along it into

● 2h – **ST. DALMAS-VALDEBLORE** 1290m (4232ft) – *limited provisions, bars/restaurants, hotels, Gîte de Valdeblore (32 places, guardian all year, bedding and kitchen equipment), campsite (500m N), telephone, buses for Nice, path junction with GR52.*

St. Dalmas possesses a very old church, situated up in the delightful old quarter – it was built in the 11th century but the crypt is 200 years older and there are 14th-century frescoes. The village makes an excellent base for walking excursions and to the E, over the Col St. Martin, is the fascinating, though more cosmopolitan, town of St. Martin-Vésubie.

GR5 leaves SE from the top of the village, by a signed track past a reservoir, up through pine forest to a spring in a clearing, then L, winding up to the

● 1h – **COL DU VARAIRE** 1710m (5610ft).

Walk along the ridge SW then bear R, gently up through the pleasant Noir woods and by a few zig-zags up to the

● 35m – **COL DU CAIRE GROS** 1906m (6253ft) – *(Col des Deux Caires on some maps), possible shelter in derelict military buildings.*

The following 11 kilometres (7 miles) of trail closely follow a mountain ridge SE and offer virtually no source of drinking water.

Dropping a little to cross a small valley, GR5 then climbs gradually across pasture below the ridge L, under Tête de Clans and round Mont Chalence, to join the ridge itself at the head of a ravine at

● 1h – **LE PERTUS** 1958m (6424ft).

Dropping slightly R again, contour below La Partissuollo and pass under a high-voltage electricity cable. There are sensational views R (SW) down to the Sainte-Anne chapel 700m (2300ft) below. The trail reaches Baisse de la Combe and a path coming up from the N. Continue SE under Cime de la Combe and, once on the ridge, follow it along and begin to enter the Manoynas forest. Fork L up small zig-zags at a path junction, crossing to the L (E) side of the ridge which rises ahead to Mont Tournairet. You soon reach another ridge (running ENE from the summit) at the

● 50m – **COLLET DES TROUS** 1982m (6502ft) – *A path R (SW) leads, in 20 mins, to Mont Tournairet 2087m (6847ft) and widespread views.*

Leave on a broad path L (E) under Cime du Fort and drop to meet an ancient track at a hairpin bend. Follow it SE for about 250 metres then follow a path S, short-cutting the track's dog-legs, down past a spring to the D332 road by a chapel. Turn R past a holiday centre in the former Tournairet military camp, now converted into

● 40m – **LES GRANGES DE LA BRASQUE** 1600m (5249ft) – *possible accommodation, provisions, water.*

Follow the road W, past a good spring (wild camping possible in the area), swinging S and climbing very gently to the

● 30m – **COL D'ANDRION** 1680m (5512ft).

Take the path straight ahead, winding downhill to meet the road again, turning R down it for a short distance before descending on a good path below it. Meet the road at two more hairpins (it continues its tortuous descent SW to the Tinée valley) and drop down on a forestry path. (Forestry work may have confused the point of departure.) Continue to the R of a low ridge in zig-zags, then along it to the

● 40m – **BOUCHE (OR COL) DES FOURNÈS** 1356m (4449ft)

Once more there is a section ahead (to Utelle) without drinking water. (A source, here, can be found in the little valley to the SE.)

Forestry activity is responsible for both the obliteration of old paths and the creation of new ones and it is possible that the trail and/or waymarking will change. Leave in a SSE direction, climbing round SW under the Tête du Planton to meet the ridge. Much of the trail is in forest, as are many of the surrounding hills. Occasionally, however, views do occur and are well worth watching out for.

Continue contouring the E slopes, round the Cîme de Bellegarde and back to the ridge at the

● 45m – **COL DE GRATTELOUP** 1411m (4629ft).

Walking down E of the Casal ridge, past ruins L, there are glimpses of rocky mountainsides. Ahead the Brec d'Utelle emerges excitingly above pastures and patches of forest. The trail climbs S over a minor ridge and takes and airy line through rocks to reach the

● 35m – **BRÈCHE DU BREC** 1520m (4987ft) – *(15 mins SE – a rocky ascent to the summit of Brec d'Utelle 1606m (5269ft), with extensive panoramas in clear conditions).*

Descend S, first over rocks then loose stones, to a beautiful viewpoint at the Col du Brec. Go round the Tête d'Escandolier, detouring W and back again, now on the W side of the ridge as the trail crosses rougher ground, fallen away in places, and reaches the Col de la Mei near the curious castle-shaped rock known as le Castel Ginestre. Continue generally S on a rough stony track, E of the rugged ridge line, then down across the tiered slopes of former cultivation to the D32 which you cross to enter

● 1h 40m – **UTELLE** 821m (2693ft) – *provisions, restaurants, hotels, car parking, telephone, Gîte d'Utelle in old church (12 places, open all year, kitchen facilities). (Follow road R at junction just before the village for the short, orange-waymarked variant to the Madonne d'Utelle sanctuary and viewpoint, a very ancient and much-frequented place of pilgrimage. Return to GR5 via the Col d'Ambellard to Chapelle Saint-Antoine.)*

Utelle is a picturesque place and, being on the old mule-track route from Nice to the Tinée valley, was at one time quite a prosperous village. Now a tourist attraction, situated as it is on a spur overlooking the Vésubie valley and the Gordolasque peaks beyond, it acts as a base for the short journey (on foot or wheels) to the Madonne d'Utelle sanctuary. The gothic St. Véran church is worthy of investigation.

From the church square, walk W then down S over a stream valley, climbing diagonally before dropping again S onto rockier hillside and SW over the steep Cros torrent valley. The gradient levels off and the trail proceeds SE over small valleys and in and out of trees, arriving at the

● 1h – **CHAPELLE SAINT-ANTOINE** 676m (2218ft).

The descent continues S, making a short detour W to cross the Rosiera valley, leading down to the Vésubie gorge below L. Turing the E corner of the Crête de la Pallu cliffs, the trail winds on down over limestone terrain to the scattered hamlet of le Cros d'Utelle at a minor road (D67). Continue SW, short-cutting the road's dog-legs and finally S down the Moutons valley to emerge at the D2565 road from Nice to St. Martin-Vésubie. Cross the road and walk R for 100m, turning L down a track to the

● 1h 20m – **PONT DU CROS** – 195m (640ft) – *buses for Nice at the road.*

This bridge spans the Vésubie river, sister to the neighbouring Tinée which it joins a few kilometres SW, together forming the broad Var flowing S to the Mediterranean. Both Tinée and Vésubie have carved out deep, rocky gorges through which roads have been audaciously cut to serve towns higher upstream like St. Etienne-de-Tinée and St. Martin-Vésubie.

Ascend bends and pass the channelled Vésubie canal, thereafter climbing an ancient track to the D19, crossing it to contour L along by a wall, with olive terraces and Levens village opposite R. Join the road again and walk L to a junction. R leads into

● **1h – LEVENS** 580m (1903ft) – *provisions, bars, restaurants, hotels, water, telephone, buses for Nice, swimming pool(!), police station, tourist information, good views from the top of the town over the Vésubie and Var, the Mediterranean coast and the snowy summits of l'Argentera, le Gelas, le Clapier and the rocky masses of the Diable and Bégo.*

GR5 turns L, spurning Levens itself, although there are the odd bar and shop along the busy road SE. Pass the D20 junction, taking the next turn R along D14 (signed 'Aspremont'). The trail turns L alongside a huge flat meadow (les Grandes Prés), the lane becoming unsurfaced. Beyond a housing development, take a path R up through thin mixed woods (blackberries galore in season). At a path junction, keep ahead, then fork L up through spiky broom and other uncomfortable species. At the hilltop, turn L then down R (not along the broad track ahead), past a ruin, descending zig-zags to the ravine bottom (some maps and guides wrong!). Contour L past olives and dwarf oaks, with Mont Cima's long ridge seen end-on ahead. The path emerges down steps onto a minor road at

● **50m – SAINTE-CLAIRE** – *buses for Nice 100m L on D19.*

Turn R for a mile to the road-end at la Lausière and take a path up L, along under the huge, sheer cliffs of sedimentary rock at Rocca Partida. At a conspicuous waymarked tree, climb L to the NE shoulder of Mont Cima 878m (2880ft), with views back to the Madonne d'Utelle. Mount the ridge SW, watching for a path off L which contours below the summit, eventually dropping though an untidy area which distinguishes itself only by virtue of a pure spring!

Walk round the small valley and join a surfaced lane, turning L along it. At a R bend on a small rise, take a path down L past a bungalow and suddenly there is a soaring view over the Var plain below. The trail threads down through spiky thickets to a road, turning

L, then R down a little unwaymarked path opposite a 'No Smoking or Camping' sign. When the road is next encountered, turn L and sharp R by a telephone in front of the spacious church square and descend the track, then the road into

● 2h – **ASPREMONT** 500m (1640ft) – *provisions, restaurants, hotels, telephone, buses for Nice and Falicon, car park. Path junction with the 'Sentiers des Balcons de la Côte d'Azur'.*

Aspremont is built on a round hill and its streets and alleys are laid out in a spiral of concentric circles. At the summit is a terrace formed by the base of the old castle.

GR5 takes the D14 road towards Nice. Just past the car park, drop R along below the road, rejoining it at a bend. Cross the road and climb a lane between houses, soon becoming a rough track. Turn up R just before a line of concrete posts, winding up through thin forest and scrub with lovely views through pine trees back to Aspremont.

Turn L up a stony path, past a ruin and in air heavy with the scent of wild mint. This delightful path contours just beneath Mont Chauve d'Aspremont's summit ridge, along hillside still patterned with once-cultivated terraces, now overgrown. Below R are the first suburban villas of Nice, their bright blue swimming pools gleaming on the arid slopes.

Crossing the descending ridge, there is a first glimpse of Nice, France's fifth largest city and even from this distance an impressive urban sprawl.

(A track L (E) leads, in 1h 45m return, to a tarred road and thence to Mont Aspremont's summit, crowned by a fort. There is, as you would expect, a first-rate panoramic view over the entire Alpes-Maritimes and Côte d'Azure.)

GR5 descends gradually S on a rocky path across scrub, crosses a broad track, passes a ruin and a pylon before reaching a popular picnic area – watch for waymarks! Pass well R of a shrine to a tarmacked path (nearly as good as a red carpet!) through semi-formal parkland. Keep L down a lane, turn R, past a bar to a drinking trough and the busy D114 at

● 2h 15m – **L'AIRE ST. MICHEL** 314m (1030ft) – *buses for Nice.*

Proceed S down the Vieux Chemin de Gairant, turning L at a

*The end of the GR5 at Nice: now you may rest!*

school, round the road hairpin and L again down the same Vieux Chemin. Cross a bridge over the A8 Autoroute, keeping straight down on a beeline for Nice and reaching Alex Médicin square in the St. Maurice district. Any avenue S brings you to the city centre and seafront of

● 1h 30m – **NICE** – *all supplies, bars, cafes, restaurants, hotels, campsites, PTT, tourist information, banks, doctors/pharmacies/hospital, bus station (Gare Routière), SNCF, taxi, airport, motorway, etc.*

There is inevitably a jolt, almost a literal 'coming down to earth', when entering a large and prosperous city after weeks, perhaps, spent on mountain paths. Chamonix, Modane and Briançon do not possess the scale to overwhelm in quite the same way as Nice; and this is, of course, the end of the trail too. Yet Nice is a fascinating city and no-one should return home without visiting the old quarter, with its honeycomb of narrow alleyways, shops and stalls; or, for that matter, the long sweep of beach, inviting you to dip a sweaty toe into the warm waters of the Mediterranean!

# SUMMARY OF GR52 VARIANT

From St. Dalmas-Valdeblore, the GR52 variant swings N, then E, in the Mercantour National Park over remote and rugged mountains to the Merveilles massif, with its prehistoric wall carvings. Still keeping to high ground and passing as near to summits as possible, there follows a long leg S on high ridges to Menton on the Mediterranean coast close to the Italian border.

Although only a short distance from the Côte d'Azur, the massifs crossed are comparable in size and terrain to any in the French Alps. In the Mercantour, the north-facing slopes of certain cols can present the walker with difficulties on account of late-lying snow and it is not rare, even at these latitudes in mid-July, to find the Merveilles lakes ice-covered in the morning.

Heat can be a problem, too, and water hard to find in the hills near the coast. Between St. Dalmas-Valdeblore and the Pointe des Trois-Communes during July and August, afternoon thunderstorms are frequent and often violent and the walker should be alert to the dangers of lightning-strike. (See section on 'Weather' in the Introduction.)

Below appears a summary of the GR52 route, containing topographical features, supply points and refuges/*gîtes* encountered.


**ST. DALMAS-VALDEBLORE** 1290m (4232ft) – *see GR5 notes.*

3h – **COL DU VEILLOS** 2194m (7198ft)

1h – **COL DU BARN** 2452m (8044ft)

1h 10m – **VACHERIE DU COLLET** 1842m (6043ft) – *water, milk, cheese.*

30m – **COL DE SALÈSE** 2031m (6663ft) – *possible camp, (45m SE – Refuge des Adus, 12 places, unguarded, bedding and kitchen equipment).*

40m – **VACHERIE DE SALÈSE** 1742m (5715ft)

1h – **BORÉON** 1473m (4833ft) – *provisions, restaurants, Gîte du Boréon, 30 places.*

1h 10m – **PONT DE PEYRESTRÈCHE** 1838m (6030ft) – *(30 mins N, Refuge de la Cougourde, 45 places, guardian 15/6 to 30/9, spring school holidays, weekends from Easter to November, bedding and kitchen equipment).*

1h – **LAC DE TRÉCOULPES** 2150m (7054ft) – *water, possible wild camp.*

50m – **PAS DES LADRES** 2448m (8031ft)

1h – **MADONE DE FENESTRE** 1903m (6243ft) – *Refuge de la Madone de Fenestre, 62 places, guardian 15/6 to 30/9 plus weekends, mattresses and blankets, wood stove, washroom and toilet; bus for St. Martin-Vésubie, Sunday evening during summer holiday.*

1h – **VALLON DU MONT-COLOMB** 2300m (7546ft)

30m – **LAC DU MONT-COLOMB** 2390m (7841ft)

45m – **PAS DU MONT-COLOMB** 2548m (8359ft)

40m – **LA BARME** 2150m (7054ft)

20m – **REFUGE NICE** 2232m (7323ft) – *Refuge de Nice, 80 places (20 in winter), guardian 15/6 to 15/10, Easter holidays, weekends and bank holidays, cooking area, meals, bedding, toilet.*

30m – **LAC NIRÉ** 2353m (7718ft)

1h 10m – **BAISSE DU BASTO** 1693m (8835ft)

1h 30m – **BAISSE DE VALMASQUE** 2549m (8363ft)

1h 15m – **REFUGE DES MERVEILLES** 2111m (6926ft) – *80 places (30 in winter) guardian 13/6 to 15/10 and weekends after Easter.*

1h 15m – **PAS DU DIABLE** 2436m (7992ft)

1h – **BAISSE CAVALINE** 2107m (6913ft)

20m – **COL DE RAUS** 1099m (3605ft)

45m – **POINTE DES TROIS COMMUNES** 2080m (6824ft)

1h – **BAISSE DE VENTABREN** 1862m (6109ft)

30m – **BAISSE DE LA DÉA** 1750m (5741ft)

1h 15m – **BAISSE DE LINIÈRE** 1346m (4416ft)

1h – **BAISSE DE FIGHIÈRE** 750m (2461ft)

1h 15m – **SOSPEL** 350m (1148ft) – *all supplies, restaurants, hotels, gîtes d'étape, campsite, PTT, tourist information, doctor/pharmacy, buses for Menton, SNCF.*

2h 15m – **COL RAZET** 1027m (3369ft)

20m – **COL DE TREITORE** 1085m (3560ft)

1h – **PRAIRIE DE MORGE** 810m (2657ft)

1h – **COL DU BERCEAU** 1090m (3576ft)

30m – **PLAN DE LION** 716m (2349ft)

1h 30m – **ROND-POINT DES COLOMBIÈRES** 110m (361ft)

15m – **GARE SNCF DE MENTON-GARAVAN** – *Menton – all supplies, bars, restaurants, hotels, campsites, PTT, tourist information, buses and trains for local and other destinations.*

# SUMMARY TABLE OF ROUTE AND TIMINGS FOR GR5 AND VARIANTS

| GR5 | Stage 1 Lac Léman to Les Houches (Chamonix valley) |
|---|---|
| | Saint-Gingolph |
| 1h 30m | Novel |
| 40m | La Planche |
| 2h | Col de Bise |
| 45m | Chalets de Bise |
| 50m | Pas de la Bosse |
| 1h 45m | La Chapelle d'Abondance |
| 2h 45m | La Torrens |
| 1h | Col des Mattes |
| 1h 30m | Lenlevay |
| 1h 15m | Col de Bassachaux |
| 1h 35m | Col de Chésery |
| 50m | Porte du Lac Vert |
| 1h 30m | Poya |
| 45m | Col de Coux |
| 2h | Col de la Golèse |
| 45m | Chalets de Bossetan |
| 1h | Les Allermands |
| 1h 15m | Moulins |
| 10m | Samoëns |
| 1h | Pont Perret |
| 1h | Le Fay |
| 20m | Salvagny |
| 45m | Cascade de Rouget |
| 40m | Chalets du Lignon |
| 45m | Cascade de Pleureuse |
| 1h | Collet d'Anterne |
| 30m | Refuge Alfred Wallis |
| 50m | Lac d'Anterne |
| 40m | Col d'Anterne |
| 30m | Chalet-Refuge de Moëde-Anterne |

| | |
|---|---|
| 1h | Pont d'Arlevé |
| 1h 15m | Path junction |
| 1h | Col du Brévent |
| 1h | Le Brévent |
| 50m | Refuge Bel-Achat |
| 50m | Merlet |
| 1h 15m | Les Houches |

### Alternative Start to the GR5

| | |
|---|---|
| | Thonon-les-Bains |
| 1h 30m | Armoy |
| 1h 30m | Reyvroz |
| 45m | Bioge |
| 40m | La Plantaz |
| 30m | Les Clouz |
| 35m | Mérou |
| 45m | Le Crêt |
| 45m | Chalets des Trables |
| 30m | Le Grand Chesnay |
| 40m | Mont Baron |
| 30m | Col des Queffaix |
| 20m | Col de la Cas d'Oche |
| 15m | Lacs d'Oche |
| 50m | Col des Portes d'Oche |
| 30m | Col de Planchamp |
| 15m | Join GR5 |

### Stage 2      Les Houches to Landry (Isère valley)

| | |
|---|---|
| 2h | Col de Voza |
| 35m | Bionnassay |
| 1h 15m | La Villette |
| 1h 40m | Les Contamines |
| 50m | Nôtre-Dame-de-la-Gorge |
| 45m | Chalet du Nant Borrant |
| 45m | Chalet-Gîte La Balme |
| 2h 15m | Col du Bonhomme |
| 50m | Col de la Croix-du-Bonhomme |
| 1h 15m | Col de la Sauce |

| | |
|---|---|
| 1h | Refuge du Plan-de-la-Laie |
| 1h | Chalet de Petite-Berge |
| 30m | Chalet de Grande-Berge |
| 1h 30m | Ruines de Presset |
| 1h 30m | Col de Bresson |
| 1h | Chalet de la Balme |
| 2h 30m | Valezan |
| 1h | Bellentre |
| 45m | Landry |

| **Stage 3** | **Landry to Modane** |
|---|---|
| 1h 30m | Peisey-Nancroix |
| 1h 30m | Refuge de Rosuel |
| 1h 30m | Chalet du Berthoud |
| 1h 15m | Chalet de la Grassaz |
| 1h 30m | Col du Palet |
| 25m | Téléski de Grattaleu, junction with GR55 |
| 1h | Lac-de-Tignes |
| 40m | Pas de la Tovière |
| 1h 45m | Val d'Isère |
| 3h 30m | Co d'Isèran |
| 45m | Pont de la Neige |
| 30m | Pied-Montet |
| 20m | Junction of GR5 and GR5E |
| 1h 15m | Chalets des Roches |
| 1h 30m | La Cabane du Molard |
| 30m | Path junction to le Villaron & GR5E |
| 30m | Bessans |
| 1h 15m | Col de la Madeleine |
| 1h | Chalets du Mollard |
| 30m | Refuge de Vallonbrun |
| 1h 50m | Refuge de Cuchet |
| 2h 30m | Chalets de la Turra de Termignon |
| 1h 30m | Parking de Bellecombe |
| 45m | Refuge du Plan du Lac |
| 30m | Torrent de la Rocheure |
| 4h | Refuge d'Arpont |
| 1h 15m | Chalets de Montafia |
| 1h 20m | Chalets de la Loza |

| 1h 20m | Chalets de la Turra |
| 1h | Télésiege du Djoin |
| 30m | La Fournache |
| 1h 30m | Col du Barbier |
| 2h | Refuge de l'Orgère |
| 45m | Ruisseau de St. Bernard |
| 1h 30m | Modane |

### GR55 Variant

| | Téléski de Grattaleu |
| 30m | Val Claret |
| 1h 30m | Junction Col de Fresse |
| 1h | Col de la Leisse |
| 1h 30m | Refuge de la Leisse |
| 1h 30m | Pont de Croé-vie |
| 45m | Ancient blockhouse |
| 1h 15m | Refuge du Col de la Vanoise |
| 1h 15m | Chalets de la Glière |
| 45m | Fontanettes |
| 20m | Pralognan-la-Vanoise |
| 45m | Pont de Gerlon |
| 1h | Pont de la Pêche |
| 2h 30m | Refuge de Péclet-Polset |
| 1h 20m | Col de Chavière |
| 45m | Path junction |
| 1h 40m | Ruisseau St. Bernard and GR5 |

### GR5E Variant

| | Path junction |
| 1h | Bonneval-sur-Arc |
| 1h 15m | Le Villaron |
| 45m | Bessans |
| 2h 30m | Lanslevillard |
| 45m | Lanslebourg-Mont-Cenis |
| 1h 30m | Termignon |
| 45m | Sollières-Sardières |
| 1h 30m | Bramans |
| 1h | Aussois |
| 1h 45m | Télésiege du Djoin and GR5 |

| Stage 4 | **Modane to Ceillac** |
|---------|-----------------------|
| 2h | Charmaix |
| 1h 10m | Chalets le Lavoir |
| 30m | Chalets la Losa |
| 1h 20m | Col de la Vallée Étroite |
| 1h 30m | Pont de la Fonderie |
| 45m | Refuge de la Vallée Étroite |
| 1h 20m | Col des Thures |
| 25m | Chalets des Thures |
| 1h 30m | Chapelle des Ames – junction with GR5C variant to Briançon |
| 1h | Plampinet |
| 1h 45m | Chalets des Acles |
| 1h 45m | Col de Dormillouse |
| 30m | Col de la Lauze |
| 2h 10m | Montgenèvre |
| 2h | Path junction – by-passing Briançon |
| 30m | Briançon |
| 1h 30m | Chalets des Ayes |
| 1h 20m | Chalets de Vers le Col |
| 45m | Col des Ayes |
| 2h | Brunissard |
| 20m | La Chalp |
| 45m | Les Maisons |
| 1h 45m | Château Queyras |
| 3h 45m | Col Fromage |
| 1h 30m | Ceillac |

| Stage 5 | **Ceillac to St. Etienne-de-Tinée** |
|---------|--------------------------------------|
| 2h | Lac des Prés-Sébeyrand |
| 1h 30m | Chapelle and Lac Sainte-Anne |
| 1h | Col Giradin |
| 1h 50m | La Barge |
| 2h | Road junction |
| 1h | Fouillouze |
| 2h | Col du Vallonnet |
| 1h 15m | Col de Mallemort |
| 2h | Larche |

| | |
|---|---|
| 1h 20m | Pont Rouge |
| 1h 40m | Lac du Lauzanier |
| 1h 25m | Pas de la Cavale |
| 40m | Lacs d'Agnel |
| 30m | Salse Morène |
| 35m | Col des Fourches |
| 45m | Bousiéyas |
| 1h 15m | Col de la Columbière |
| 1h 50m | St. Dalmas-le-Selvage |
| 1h | Col d'Anelle |
| 1h 10m | St. Etienne-de-Tinée |

## Stage 6      St. Etienne-de-Tinée to Nice

| | |
|---|---|
| 2h | Auron |
| 1h 15m | Col du Blainon |
| 1h 10m | Roya |
| 3h 45m | Col de Crousette |
| 1h 30m | Col de Mulinés |
| 1h 35m | Gîte de Longon |
| 1h 10m | Rougios |
| 1h 15m | Roure |
| 1h | St. Sauveur-sur-Tinée |
| 1h 30m | Rimplas |
| 2h | St. Dalmas-Valdeblore |
| 1h | Col du Varaire |
| 35m | Col du Caire Gros |
| 1h | Le Pertus |
| 50m | Collet des Trous |
| 40m | Les Granges de la Brasque |
| 30m | Col d'Andrion |
| 40m | Bouche des Fournès |
| 45m | Col de Gratteloup |
| 35m | Brèche du Brec |
| 1h 40m | Utelle |
| 1h | Chapelle Saint-Antoine |
| 1h 20m | Pont du Cros |
| 1h | Levens |
| 50m | Sainte-Claire |
| 2h | Aspremont |

| 2h 15m | L'Aire St. Michel |
| 1h 30m | Nice |

## GR52 Variant from St. Dalmas-Valdeblore to Menton

| 3h | Col du Veillos |
| 1h | Col du Barn |
| 1h 10m | Vacherie du Collet |
| 30m | Col de Salèse |
| 40m | Vacherie de Salèse |
| 1h | Boréon |
| 1h 10m | Pont de Peyrestrèche |
| 1h | Lac de Trécoulpes |
| 50m | Pas des Ladres |
| 1h | Madone de Fenestre |
| 1h | Vallon du Mont-Colomb |
| 30m | Lac du Mont-Colomb |
| 45m | Pas du Mont-Colomb |
| 40m | La Barme |
| 20m | Refuge Nice |
| 30m | Lac Niré |
| 1h 10m | Baisse du Basto |
| 1h 30m | Baisse de Valmasque |
| 1h 15m | Refuge des Merveilles |
| 1h 15m | Pas du Diable |
| 1h | Baisse Cavaline |
| 20m | Col de Raus |
| 45m | Pointe des Trois Communes |
| 1h | Baisse de Ventabren |
| 30m | Baisse de la Déa |
| 1h 15m | Baisse de Linière |
| 1h | Baisse de Fighière |
| 1h 15m | Sospel |
| 2h 15m | Col Razet |
| 20m | Col de Treitore |
| 1h | Prairie de Morge |
| 20m | Col du Berceau |
| 30m | Plan de Lion |
| 1h 30m | Rond-Point des Colombières |
| 15m | SNCF Menton-Garavan |

# A SELECTION OF CICERONE GUIDES

## WALKING AND TREKKING IN THE ALPS

### WALKING IN THE ALPS
*Kev Reynolds*

The popular author of many of our Alpine guidebooks now draws on his vast experience to produce an outstanding comprehensive volume. Every area covered. Not for over half a century has there been anything remotely comparable. Fully illustrated.
*ISBN 1 85284 261 X Large format Case bound 496pp*

### 100 HUT WALKS IN THE ALPS
*Kev Reynolds*

A fine introduction to Europe's highest mountains and to life in the excellent network of Alpine huts. From southern France, through Switzerland, Austria and Italy to Slovenia. Printed in full colour.
*ISBN 1 85284 297 0*

### CHAMONIX TO ZERMATT - The Walker's Haute Route
*Kev Reynolds*

The classic walk in the shadow of great peaks from Mont Blanc to the Matterhorn. In 14 stages, this is one of the most beautiful LD paths in Europe.
*ISBN 1 85284 215 6 176pp*

### THE GRAND TOUR OF MONTE ROSA
*C.J. Wright*

The ultimate alpine LD walk which encircles most of the Pennine Alps.

#### Vol 1: MARTIGNY TO VALLE DELLA SESIA (via the Italian valleys)
*ISBN 1 85284 177 X 216pp PVC cover*

#### Vol 2: VALLE DELLA SESIA TO MARTIGNY (via the Swiss valleys)
*ISBN 1 85284 178 8 182pp PVC cover*

### TOUR OF MONT BLANC
*Andrew Harper*

One of the world's best walks - the circumnavigation of the Mont Blanc massif. 120 miles of pure magic, split into 11 sections. Reprinted and updated.
*ISBN 1 85284 240 7 144pp PVC cover*

## FRANCE, BELGIUM AND LUXEMBOURG

### WALKING IN THE ARDENNES
*Alan Castle*

53 circular walks in this attractive area of gorges and deep-cut wooded valleys, caves, castles and hundreds of walking trails. Easily accessible from the channel.
*ISBN 1 85284 213 X 312pp*

### CHAMONIX - MONT BLANC - A Walking Guide
*Martin Collins*

In the dominating presence of Europe's highest mountain, the scenery is exceptional. A comprehensive guide to the area.
*ISBN 1 85284 009 9 192pp PVC cover*

### WALKING IN THE ECRINS NATIONAL PARK
*Kev Reynolds*

Containing some spectacularly beautiful scenery, the Ecrins offer huge potential. Kev describes numerous routes for most abilities, together with maps and other local information.
*ISBN 1 85284 322 5 £TBA PVC cover*

### WALKING THE FRENCH GORGES
*Alan Castle*

320 miles through Provence and Ardèche. Includes the famous gorges of the Verdon.
*ISBN 1 85284 114 1 224pp*

**FRENCH ROCK** *Bill Birkett*

THE guide to many exciting French crags! Masses of photo topos, with selected hit-routes in detail.
*ISBN 1 85284 113 3 332pp A5 size*

**WALKING IN THE HAUTE SAVOIE** *Janette Norton*

61 walks in the pre-Alps of Chablais, to majestic peaks in the Faucigny, Haut Giffre and Lake Annecy regions.
*ISBN 1 85284 196 6 312pp*

**WALKING IN THE LANGUEDOC** *John Cross*

31 walks in the stunningly beautiful Parc Naturel du Haut-Languedoc. The climate is warm, the vineyards stretch out below you, and above is the towering Massif.
*ISBN 1 85284 309 8*

**TOUR OF THE OISANS: GR54** *Andrew Harper*

This popular walk around the Dauphiné massif and Écrins national park is similar in quality to the celebrated Tour of Mont Blanc. A two-week suggested itinerary covers the 270km route.
*ISBN 1 85284 157 5 120pp PVC cover*

**WALKING IN PROVENCE** *Janette Norton*

42 walks through the great variety of Provence - remote plateaux, leafy gorges, ancient villages, monuments, quiet towns. Provence is evocative of a gentler life.
*ISBN 1 85284 293 8 248pp*

**THE PYRENEAN TRAIL: GR10** *Alan Castle*

From the Atlantic to the Mediterranean at a lower level than the Pyrenean High Route. 50 days - but splits into holiday sections.
*ISBN 1 85284 245 8 176pp*

**THE TOUR OF THE QUEYRAS** *Alan Castle*

A 13-day walk which traverses wild but beautiful country, the sunniest part of the French Alps. Suitable for a first Alpine visit.
*ISBN 1 85284 048 X 160pp*

**THE ROBERT LOUIS STEVENSON TRAIL** *Alan Castle*

140 mile trail in the footsteps of Stevenson's *Travels with a Donkey* through the Cevennes from Le Puy to St Jean du Gard. This route is ideal for people new to walking holidays.
*ISBN 1 85284 060 9 160pp*

## FRANCE/SPAIN

**WALKING IN THE TARENTAISE AND BEAUFORTAIN ALPS** *J.W. Akitt*

The delectable mountain area south of Mont Blanc includes the Vanoise National Park. 53 day walks, 5 tours between 2 and 8 days' duration, plus 40 short outings.
*ISBN 1 85284 181 8 216pp*

**ROCK CLIMBS IN THE VERDON - An Introduction** *Rick Newcombe*

An English-style guide, which makes for easier identification of the routes and descents.
*ISBN 1 85284 015 3 72pp*

**TOUR OF THE VANOISE** *Kev Reynolds*

A 10-12 day circuit of one of the finest mountain areas of France, between Mt Blanc and the Écrins. The second most popular mountain tour after the Tour of Mont Blanc.
*ISBN 1 85284 224 5 120pp*

**WALKS IN VOLCANO COUNTRY** *Alan Castle*

Two LD walks in Central France, the High Auvergne and Tour of the Velay, in a unique landscape of extinct volcanoes.
*ISBN 1 85284 092 7 208pp*

**ROCK CLIMBS IN THE PYRENEES**           *Derek Walker*

Includes Pic du Midi d'Ossau and the Vignemale in France, and the Ordesa Canyon and Riglos in Spain.

*ISBN 1 85284 039 0  168pp  PVC cover*

**WALKS AND CLIMBS IN THE PYRENEES**           *Kev Reynolds*

Includes the Pyrenean High Level Route. Invaluable for any backpacker or mountaineer who plans to visit this still unspoilt mountain range. (3rd Edition)

*ISBN 1 85284 133 8  328pp  PVC cover*

**THE WAY OF ST JAMES: Le Puy to Santiago - A Cyclist's Guide**     *John Higginson*

This guide for touring cyclists follows as closely as possible the original route but avoids the almost unrideable sections of the walkers' way.  On surfaced lanes and roads.

*ISBN 1 85284 274 1  112pp*

**THE WAY OF ST JAMES: Le Puy to Santiago - A Walker's Guide**     *Alison Raju*

A walker's guide to the ancient route of pilgrimage.  Plus the continuation to Finisterre.

*ISBN 1 85284 271 7  264pp*

# SWITZERLAND

**ALPINE PASS ROUTE, SWITZERLAND**           *Kev Reynolds*

Over 15 passes along the northern edge of the Alps, past the Eiger, Jungfrau and many other renowned peaks.  A 325 km route in 15 suggested stages.

*ISBN 1 85284 069 2  176pp*

**THE BERNESE ALPS, SWITZERLAND**           *Kev Reynolds*

Walks around Grindelwald, Lauterbrunnen and Kandersteg dominated by the great peaks of the Oberland.

*ISBN 1 85284 243 1  248pp  PVC cover*

**CENTRAL SWITZERLAND - A Walking Guide**           *Kev Reynolds*

A little known but delightful area stretching from Luzern to the St Gotthard. Includes Engelberg and Klausen Pass.

*ISBN 1 85284 131 1  216pp  PVC cover*

**WALKS IN THE ENGADINE, SWITZERLAND**           *Kev Reynolds*

The superb region to the south-east of Switzerland of the Bregaglia, Bernina Alps and the Engadine National Park.

*ISBN 1 85284 003 X  192pp  PVC cover*

**THE JURA: WALKING THE HIGH ROUTE and WINTER SKI TRAVERSES**    *Kev Reynolds, R. Brian Evans*

The High Route is a long distance path along the highest crest of the Swiss Jura.  In winter it is a paradise for cross-country skiers.  Both sections in one volume.

*ISBN 1 85284 010 2  192pp*

**WALKING IN TICINO, SWITZERLAND**           *Kev Reynolds*

Walks in the lovely Italian part of Switzerland, surprisingly little known to British walkers.

*ISBN 1 85284 098 6  184pp  PVC cover*

**THE VALAIS, SWITZERLAND - A Walking Guide**           *Kev Reynolds*

The splendid scenery of the Pennine Alps, with such peaks as the Matterhorn, Dent Blanche and Mont Rosa providing a perfect background.

*ISBN 1 85284 151 6  224pp  PVC cover*

**International Distress Signal**
(*Only to be used in an emergency*)

Six blasts on a whistle (and flashes with a torch after dark) spaced
evenly for one minute, followed by a minute's pause.
Repeat until an answer is received. The response is three signals
per minute followed by a minute's pause.

The following signals are used to communicate with a helicopter:

**Help needed:**
raise both arms
above head to
form a 'V'

**Help not required:**
raise one arm above
head, extend other
arm downward

In an emergency the mountain rescue (*secours en montagne*)
can be called on 04 92 22 22 22
*Note: mountain rescues must be paid for – be insured*

# EXPLORE THE WORLD
# WITH A CICERONE GUIDE

Cicerone publishes over 280 guides for walking, trekking, climbing
and exploring the UK, Europe and worldwide. Cicerone guides are
available from outdoor shops, quality book stores and from the publisher.

**Cicerone can be contacted on**
**Tel. 01539 562069**
**Fax: 01539 563417**
**www.cicerone.co.uk**